ALCOHOLISM:

New Light on the Disease

ALCOHOLISM:

New Light on the Disease

John Wallace

Edgehill
Publications

ALCOHOLISM: New Light on the Disease

Published in the United States by Edgehill Publications, 200 Harrison Avenue, Newport, RI 02840

Library of Congress Cataloging in Publication Data

Wallace, John.
    Alcoholism: New Light on the Disease.

    References and recommended reading: p. 149
    Includes index.
    1. Alcoholism.   2. Alcoholism recovery.   3. Alcoholism treatment.
    4. Disease concept of alcoholism.   Sobriety. I. Title.

ISBN 0-933741-01-4

First Edition

LC 85-80595

Produced by Lexis Press, Chapel Hill, NC

Table of Contents

Preface

In the several decades during which I have been active in the field of alcoholism, I have thought about writing a book to be read by alcoholic people themselves as well as by the professionals who research the disease and treat it. A host of reasons always appeared to dissuade me. For one thing, Alcoholics Anonymous had already managed the job very well without me. The book *Alcoholics Anonymous* and the various writings of Bill Wilson seemed to address aspects of the disease and recovery in a manner that didn't leave much room for improvement.

For another thing, the press of my clinical work and writing kept me involved with writing for professionals—I wrote numerous clinical papers and articles, and edited and wrote much of a major report to the United States Congress on alcohol and health. But I never did seem to find time to write a book for the people who suffer from this disease.

However, as I read more deeply in such areas as the genetic basis, the chemistry of alcoholism, and as I extended my knowledge about such things as the neurobiology of depression and anxiety, I became more and more convinced that I had something to say to alcoholic people themselves. But it wasn't only my scientific knowledge that had grown in eighteen years of activity in the field, my development as a psychological and spiritual creature had come farther along the path too. My enthusiasm for a book on alcoholism grew as I considered the possibility that I might also have something of value to say to those persons interested in higher powers, personal growth, surrender, and powerlessness.

Much of this book deals with the disease itself as well as recovery from it, as does the famous *Alcoholics Anonymous.* These two books—these two bodies of knowledge—are entirely compatible with each other. Understanding the genetic basis of alcoholism and knowing what is happening in our brains supports our resolve to stay sober. At the same time, our experience as recovering alcoholics and our personal growth in sobriety shed light on the nature of this disease and its many facets.

I don't pretend for a moment that I've written all there is to be said about alcoholism in this book. The disease is truly astonishing. As members of Alcoholics Anonymous are quick to point out, the disease is cunning, baffling, and powerful. It is all these and more too.

In writing this book I've tried to be selective rather than comprehensive; I've tried to resist the temptation to treat a topic exhaustively. While comprehensiveness and exhaustive treatments are appropriate to academic writing, these virtues are likely to prove impossible obstacles to readers seeking larger understandings rather than appreciation of small detail. I've tried to give the reader the relevant point of some area of discussion rather than all the points it is possible to give.

If this book succeeds in explaining the disease concept of alcoholism to those who have to date shut their minds to impressive scientific evidence, that will be most gratifying. But more importantly, if it helps one alcoholic to choose sobriety over continued drinking, then it will have served its purpose admirably.

Finally, I would like to express my appreciation to the several thousand alcoholics I have known and cared about over the years. Without their expert instruction of me, this book would not have been possible.

J. W.
Newport, Rhode Island and
Westchester County, New York

To Chester H. Kirk—
friend, trusted colleague,
and dedicated worker for sobriety

CHAPTER 1

The Disease is Costly

Alcoholism can be a devastating disease. We can see this readily if we give our full attention to the worlds about us and try to see these worlds with new clarity.

If we live in the city, an attentive walk on the streets in certain parts of town will provide us with evidence of the extent to which this cruel condition can ravage the human personality and spirit. There on the streets of our large urban centers we are likely to witness the end-state of the unchecked progression of this disease. To some, these suffering people are "bums." Others refer to them as "drunks," or perhaps "derelicts." To still others, they are "chronic alcoholics," "inhabitants of Skid Road," or "public inebriates."

But whatever we choose to call these desperately ill people who live in the doorways, subways, and back alleys of our cities, we dare not forget that they are human beings very much like ourselves. These late-stage alcoholics actually make up only three to five percent of the alcoholic population. They are people whose productive lives and social reputations have been torn apart by alcoholism. The vast majority of alcoholics, however, are not on the streets, but are functioning in society. They are manning our corporations, teaching our children, practicing law, doing surgery, flying airplanes, writing our novels, making our cars, and so forth.

While the awesome impact of alcoholism is apparent on our streets, it is even more evident in our hospitals. By current estimates, health care in America consumes nearly ten percent of our gross national product. Of these dollars going for health care, many are directly attributable to the disease of alcoholism. A recent study by the Research Triangle Institute for the National Alcohol, Drug Abuse, and Mental Health Administration revealed that the total economic costs of alcohol abuse to American society in 1983 amounted to $116.7 billion. By way of contrast, drug abuse costs the American public $59.7 billion, and mental health problems, $72.8 billion. Many of these total economic costs of alcohol abuse are accounted for by the significant role that alcoholism plays in rising health-care costs.

As studies have shown, large numbers of visits to emergency rooms and admissions to general hospitals are the result of alcoholism and problem drinking. In our emergency rooms, at least a quarter of traumatic injuries received from mishaps such as motor vehicle crashes, falls, fights, burns, recreational accidents, and gunshot wounds are alcohol-related.

A series of studies in New York City in the 1970s showed just how costly alcoholism is in the health care systems. At St. Vincent's Hospital in Manhattan, study of all male admissions to the medical-surgical unit revealed that over half of the men had serious drinking problems. Most of these men were not diagnosed as suffering from alcoholism, nor treated for alcoholism. What they were diagnosed and treated for were the medical complications or outcomes of alcoholism: liver disease, pancreatitis, heart disease, high blood pressure, disorders of the brain and motor nerves, traumatic injuries, and other diseases that follow in the wake of alcoholism with alarming frequency.

That the situation at St. Vincent's Hospital at this time was not unique was shown by two other New York City studies, one at Harlem Hospital and the other at the Hospital for Joint Diseases and Medical Center. In both of these large health-care facilities, roughly 60 percent of the male and 30 percent of the female patients in general medical services had drinking problems. Once again, the drinking problems were for the most part not commented upon, and a diagnosis of alcoholism had not been made.

On the nation's highways the tragic toll of alcoholism and problem drinking is vaguely but not fully grasped. Most people know that the drinking and driving problem is serious, but many do not appreciate just how serious it is. A few statistics are in order. Every two years, more Americans are killed on the nation's highways than were killed in the entire Vietnam war. At least half of the fatal car crashes in America involve alcohol. In terms of money, the costs of alcohol-related motor vehicle crashes are now over three billion dollars a year.

These awful numbers do not lie, but they only partially reveal the extent of our problem. Whether they realize it or not, alcoholics who continue to drink are usually walking on the edge of disaster. Marriages crack and fall apart with depressing regularity for alcoholics. Jobs and careers may come to sudden premature ends. Houses are lost, friends grow alienated, money is made and lost, children become confused and resentful, and neighbors turn away. Over it all hangs an omnipresent, heavy cloud of pessimism, sorrow, loneliness, and feelings of impending doom. There may be scrapes with the law over such things as driving while intoxicated. Arguments with the boss (or with subordinates if the alcoholic is the boss) are not uncommon. Increasingly sullen silences or open rages in the home from spouses who previously gave of themselves unselfishly are part of the terrible lot of the alcoholic.

Of course, all of these things may not happen to every alcoholic. But the fact is that they occur with such frequency among alcoholics as to lead us to believe that they are fairly common happenings in alcoholic lives, not unusual events.

Alcoholism is indeed a cruel condition. Left to run its course, it can ravage the body and bring about ruinous social consequences. Its collision with the human personality robs us of our self-esteem, blunts the sharp edges of our uniqueness, and mocks our potentialities. In its wake, there is often meaninglessness, sorrow that goes beyond our understanding, and loss of purpose to our lives.

As the various reports to the United States Congress on Alcohol and Health from the National Institute on Alcohol Abuse and Alcoholism have pointed out, alcoholism can be a deadly disease. Alcoholics have been found to be ten times more likely to die in a fire than are nonalcoholics, and 50 percent of adult fire deaths have been found to involve alcohol. Half of those who die from falls each year have been drinking heavily. With regard to suicide, studies have shown that as many as 64 percent of attempted suicides and 30 percent of actual suicides involve alcohol. Alcohol shortens the lives of many people by at least ten years.

Despite these grim statistics, however, there is hope. Alcoholics in ever increasing numbers are discovering that recovery from this dread disease is not only possible but probable if workable programs of understanding and action are energetically pursued and maintained.

There are reasons today to be optimistic about our chances for recovery. The stigma previously associated with the disease is steadily diminishing, while stereotype and misunderstanding are being replaced by reliable information and genuine social concern. Moreover, alcoholism, along with many other diseases that have plagued human beings, is finally being carefully scrutinized in laboratories around the world. In the past fifteen years, a great deal of scientific and clinical information bearing on alcoholism has exploded from the world's leading educational and scientific institutions. While we are still far from a complete understanding of alcoholism, significant strides forward have happened in the last decade alone.

Alcoholics need not be without hope. Today, throughout the world, there are millions of people who once suffered from this dread disease but who are now leading sober, productive, and reasonably happy lives. We must put pessimism aside. Alcoholics do recover from alcoholism. They do get well. Their families do find freedom from the trap of active alcoholism in their midst.

If the past six decades have taught us anything at all about alcoholism, it is this message of hope. Alcoholism may be a disease of great sorrow and suffering, but it is not a hopeless condition. Understood properly and dealt with appropriately, alcoholism is a beatable illness.

For every alcoholic there is always hope of recovery.

CHAPTER 2

Alcoholism Doesn't Make Sense

In addition to being a devastating disease, alcoholism is also a confusing one. Many people don't realize that they have this life-threatening illness until it is almost too late to do anything about it. If we are fortunate enough to be able to strip away the denial that often goes with alcoholism, we do get glimpses of where the disease has taken us and where we are heading. Such moments of clarity, however, occur infrequently for drinking alcoholics. A characteristic blindness to what alcohol has done to us and to those around us is more often the rule.

Alcoholism doesn't make sense to its victims. For many alcoholics, it is an on again – off again problem. Not every day is spent drinking and not every drinking day ends in intoxication or disaster. While it is true that an alcoholic drinking bout must begin with a first drink, it would be misleading for anyone to interpret this truism to mean that one drink will necessarily trigger off a disastrous drinking episode in every alcoholic. Alcoholics need to be counseled to stay away from alcohol in any form or amount not because they will immediately become intoxicated if they have a drink, but because more likely they won't! That is one of several reasons why the disease is often referred to as insidious. Many alcoholics will try to "prove" to themselves that they are not alcoholics by having a drink or two on given occasions and letting it go at that. They seem to be successful at this self-deceptive act. But if we were to follow these alcoholics over a period of time, we would very likely find that their "proof" is short-lived, and eventually their drinking will once again result in uncontrolled intoxication and personal disaster. These addicts are the episodic or "binge" drinkers who go in and out of devastating bouts with alcohol. Because of the episodic nature of their drinking problem, these alcoholics often have a great deal of difficulty in seeing the reality of their alcoholism.

While many alcoholics go in and out of terrible drinking episodes, there are other alcoholics who cannot tolerate even a small amount of alcohol without arousing the urge to become intoxicated. For these alcoholics, one drink will always be one too many, since virtually every drinking episode results in intoxication, disordered actions, or problematic social behavior.

There are, of course, alcoholics who drink daily. For these alcoholics, the disease is as confusing as it is for the episodic or binge drinker, but for a different reason. Many daily drinking alcoholics develop such elevated levels of physiological tolerance to the drug that while their blood alcohol levels may be quite high, you wouldn't know it by their behavior. Alcoholics of this type are sometimes referred to as "glow" drinkers; their drinking seems to be directed toward the maintenance of a given level of intoxication. This desired level of intoxication is a steady state, an "alcoholic glow" that the drinker seeks to preserve and maintain.

Since these daily maintenance drinkers are often quietly drinking themselves to death over many years, they do not call attention to themselves as do the loud, boisterous, and socially reckless alcoholics. Hence, they may not come into conflict with the law, on the job, or in their neighborhoods until their alcoholism has progressed to serious proportions. Very often the damage being done is internal, as alcohol attacks and systematically destroys major organ systems of the body. Alcoholism of this type is truly an insidious illness, silently destroying its victims who are often unaware of what is happening to them. Typically, maintenance drinkers have difficulty seeing their drinking as a problem. It is often the aware physician who, upon detecting an enlarged liver on physical examination or uncovering some other alcohol-related illness, will first call attention to a possible problem with alcohol.

Differences in drinking patterns, then, are one source of confusion about alcoholism. Some of these patterns fit widely held stereotypes, but a very large number do not.

Choice of beverage is still another potential source of confusion to the person who suffers unknowingly from the disease. Many alcoholics simply do not believe that they can be alcoholics since they "never touch the hard stuff." They drink only beer, or fine French burgundies, or perhaps even homemade wines and fruit cordials. For these persons, alcoholics are people who drink "hard" beverages such as gin, rye, scotch, bourbon, vodka and so forth.

The truth, of course, is that all alcoholic beverages contain alcohol, and it is the alcohol that is the issue here, not the beverage in which it is contained. It is possible that allergies to the hops, yeasts, fruits, grains, and other vegetable matters from which different alcoholic beverages are produced may be involved in some persons' reactions to alcohol. But as far as alcoholism is concerned, the vast majority of scientific authorities agree that alcohol and its metabolic breakdown products are the crucial elements, not the type of beverage.

In short, alcoholics can and do drink anything—beer, wine, spirits, cordials, gin, vodka, and anything else that contains alcohol.

Quantity of drinking is still another source of confusion. While it is true that alcoholics tend to drink larger quantities of alcohol than do non-alcoholics, this isn't always the case. Some alcoholics do not have to drink often, not do they have to drink very large quantities, before they find themselves in trouble with alcohol.

Women, for example, may have serious alcohol problems, but in comparison with larger and heavier males, they may drink far less. The aging brain may show diminishing tolerance to alcohol, so the elderly alcoholic may show problematic behavior after relatively small amounts of alcohol. Teenage alcoholics with very limited and brief experiences with alcohol may also show extremely disordered behavior in response to very few drinks. Alcoholics on certain medications for chronic health conditions may be able to drink only a little before showing the effects. In effect, heavy drinking, while certainly a useful thing to take into account, is not an infallible sign of alcoholism.

Heavy drinking is, in and of itself, not ever a good thing. Alcohol is a dangerous drug, and heavy drinkers are clearly at risk for alcohol-related injury and disease. Hence, heavy drinking should always be taken seriously, and efforts should be made to moderate such drinking, if possible, or to stop it entirely. However, the absence of heavy drinking cannot be taken to mean that alcoholism is not a possibility.

If patterns of drinking, type of beverage, and amount of drinking are not totally reliable guides for persons honestly seeking to understand their true conditions, what else can be considered? A focus on *consequences* is one helpful way to look at things. Instead of asking, "How much do I drink?" or "How often do I drink?" the person might try asking, "What happens when I drink?"

The person must be prepared to be honest in answering, for nothing will come of the question if it is not asked with honest intent. The question should also be asked with some patience. All the consequences of our drinking will not be apparent to us immediately, since human memory tends to be much clouded by our tendencies to protect ourselves from blame, guilt, anxiety, and shame. But if we are able to put aside our defensiveness momentarily and to ask our question with some humility, the answers are usually forthcoming. For most of us who are alcoholics, the footprints of alcoholism are there in the myriad trails of our lives. And like archeologists of our own pasts, a bit of digging is quite likely to unearth more than a few negative results of our drinking.

Since the experience of blackouts is one of the first signs of impending trouble with alcoholism, we should first ask if our drinking led to these losses of memory. If we can remember waking up after a drinking bout and having no luck at all in remembering what happened after a certain point the night before, that is evidence of a blackout. Driving from a bar to our homes and not remembering the drive is a blackout, as is having a conversation with someone and not remembering we did so.

Blackouts can range from momentary losses of recall to losses of an entire evening's worth of memories, or even several days, as has happened in some cases. The fact that we may not recall what happened during a blackout does not mean that we were unconscious. Alcoholics *function* during blackouts. They walk around, talk to others, drive cars, eat meals, sign contracts, make commitments, go to dances, have sex, and so forth. The trouble is that they don't remember much of it.

Not all alcoholics will show this early symptom of alcoholism. If you are wondering about yourself, it is important to note that the absence of blackouts does *not* mean you are not an alcoholic.

Relationships are another way to recognize alcoholism in ourselves. If we are parents, trouble with our children often goes hand in hand with our drinking. For married alcoholics, the marital relationship is invariably complicated to some degree or another by the disease. Drinking leads to conflicts with friends, lovers, associates on the job, and even strangers we meet in a bar, at a party, or on the streets. *If our drinking is causing us trouble in our basic human relationships, we must take seriously the possibility that we may have fallen victim to the disease of alcoholism.*

Scrapes with the law are another common result of drinking that may point to alcoholism. An arrest for driving while impaired or for drunken driving should certainly motivate persons to devote some serious thought to their drinking. If our drinking behavior causes us to come to the attention of the police for any reason at all, this should be a signal that something is wrong. It goes without saying that arrest and conviction for any serious crime committed while intoxicated is evidence that almost nobody will be able to ignore.

While some alcoholics are financially successful despite their alcoholism, others are plunged into financial ruin and bankruptcy. Drinking alcoholics are often foolish about their money and throw it about recklessly. They may throw away their savings on an unrealistic and ill-advised investment venture, or they may get sued for everything they have. These negative financial consequences of drinking are further information to which a person should attend.

Finally, grave personal health consequences—in the form of alcohol-related accidents and diseases—should send up "red alerts" to the person that alcoholism is likely the cause. Cirrhosis of the liver, for example, is an illness that in a heavy drinker is most likely a result of alcoholism. Similarly, although pancreatitis has other causes, alcoholism is the most likely cause when it occurs in a person who drinks frequently and heavily. Crashes, near drownings, boating mishaps, fights, light plane crashes, home fires, falls, and injuries from improper use of tools, weapons, and utensils are a few of the more dramatic results that often go with alcoholism.

In addition to looking at what our drinking is doing to us, we might consider certain "signs" that have been associated with alcoholism. Gulping drinks hurriedly rather than sipping them leisurely is sometimes a sign of the disease. So are the following: inner shakiness the day after a drinking bout; tremor or shaking hands; drinking in the morning; making up excuses for drinking to excess; hiding bottles at work or in the house; stopping drinking entirely for periods of time.

Preoccupation with alcoholic beverages and drinking situations is clearly a danger sign. If we often find ourselves thinking about drinking and devising plans either to go to or to make drinking situations happen, this should provide warning. People do, of course, give and go to parties in order to meet others and to have pleasant social interchanges with friends. But if drinking is the big attraction of parties for us, then that fact should be faced honestly.

Occasional loss of control over how much we drink or how we behave while drinking is a serious sign, one that can be ignored only at considerable risk to ourselves. If we cannot consistently guarantee our drinking behavior or our personal and social behavior while drinking, we are truly in a dangerous situation. Out-of-control alcoholics have wrecked cars, gotten themselves involved with people they should have stayed far away from, killed themselves or other people, hurt their spouses and children, and made fools of themselves on the job, in their neighborhoods, and in social relationships generally. By failing to exercise restraint, out-of-control alcoholics have made enemies out of friends and placed themselves at a disadvantage in personal and business dealings with others. Considering all that can happen to an out-of-control person in this world, we must not be deceived into thinking that occasional losses of personal control due to uncontrolled drinking are simply harmless fun. Such episodes could cost us our self-respect or even our lives.

While any loss of control over our drinking and our behavior while drinking is serious, frequent or consistent loss of control is an ominous sign. If we find ourselves often ending up drunk when we intended to have only a few drinks, we are already in deep trouble with alcohol. And if we find ourselves doing things that are not at all in accord with our fundamental, core values, then we had better come to grips with our alcohol problems immediately.

In the final analysis, the following definition of alcoholism can be helpful: *Alcoholics are people who cannot consistently control their drinking over time, and who cannot guarantee their personal and social behavior once they start to drink.*

CHAPTER 3

The Illness is Fourfold

The origin of alcoholism is still a scientific mystery. Precisely why one drinker will fall victim to the disease while another will continue to enjoy a lifetime of moderate, nonproblem drinking is not known with certainty. We do know that it isn't a matter of sinners versus saints. Alcoholics aren't bad people trying to be good people. They are ill people trying to get well.

Alcoholics are not sinners, and they are not persons of weak character and will; nor are they necessarily mentally ill people. Alcoholism is not a mental illness, nor a disease of character. Despite public opinion to the contrary, a large amount of objective, scientific research has failed to demonstrate the existence of an "alcoholic personality pattern" that precedes the onset of the disease and drives the person into destructive drinking.

For the most part, active alcoholics tend to be anything but weak-willed. Many are actually strong-willed to a fault. Stubborn, grandiose, resistant to the opinions of others and defiant, they are often their own worst enemies. Of course, we must be careful not to generalize too widely, since alcoholics are not all alike. Moreover, the personality features that we see among alcoholics are more likely to be the *results* of the disease and not its causes. Alcoholism has an awesome impact on the human being—mind as well as body. It isn't likely that the disease will wreak havoc on the liver and the central nervous system, but spare the human personality.

While science doesn't yet have *all* the answers about alcoholism and its origins, this does not mean that nothing of value is known. Promising leads from scientific research have come from international laboratories in the past decade alone, and useful ways of looking at the disease have been available to us for many years.

Alcoholism is a fourfold illness. It is physical, psychological, social, and spiritual. Any attempt to explain the illness that leaves out one or more of these factors is incomplete. Every alcoholic has a body as well as a mind, exists in a particular social context, and can be seen as striving to find meaning and purpose in a life that often seems devoid of these qualities. Even though the manner in which these four factors interact to produce alcoholism is still not clear, most authorities agree that the answers lie in the interplay between and among biology, psychology, society, and the spirit.

One of the first sophisticated views of alcoholism came out of the work of the early members of Alcoholics Anonymous and their nonalcoholic professional advisors. Dr. William Silkworth, a nonalcoholic physician active in the field of alcoholism earlier in this century, believed that alcoholism was an allergy of the body to alcohol coupled with an obsession of the mind. Dr. Silkworth's explanation was a *psychosomatic* one in that he saw two factors operating in the illness, one physical and the other psychological.

It would be difficult to fault Dr. Silkworth's ideas about the alcoholic's obsession with alcohol. The preoccupation with drinking and drinking situations is easily documented by even the most casual observations of alcoholic people. The allergy hypothesis, however, has not been so readily proved by empirical observations. But as with many things scientific, and just as widespread doubt about the role of allergy in alcoholism has gained favor, new evidence and thinking have reopened the question. Dr. Theron Randolph, one of the world's pioneer scientists concerned with the role of allergies in the mental, emotional, and behavioral problems of human beings, has pointed to the possible significance of allergy in alcoholism. This work has been further elaborated by specialists in allergy and behavior called *clinical ecologists.* Dr. Richard Mackarness, a British psychiatrist and clinical ecologist, is interested in the fact that alcoholic beverages are commonly made from cereal grains: wheat, rye, barley, and corn. Allergies to these particular cereal grains are common. Dr. Randolph believes corn to be the most widespread allergenic foodstuff, while allergies to wheat are frequent. In effect, when we drink alcoholic beverages we also risk exposure to vegetable matter to which we may be allergic. Moreover, many specialists now believe that the more we eat or drink of a particular food, the more likely it is that we will develop an allergic sensitivity to it. For some people, daily consumption of a particular food, or even frequent consumption, practically insures eventual sensitivity.

But if alcoholics are, in fact, allergic to the various substances from which alcoholic beverages are made, how could this lead to addiction? One would think that the allergic reaction would put them off the beverages altogether—not lead to compulsive use. There are two answers to this question; one concerns the concept of *masking*, and the other is involved with the body's *general adaptation response to stress*.

As Dr. Herbert J. Rinkel hypothesized over twenty years ago, many of us are victims of undetected food allergies that began in childhood or infancy and were transformed without our awareness as we grew older. What might have begun as indigestion and diarrhea in an infant in response to a milk allergy may show up in adulthood as hives or asthma on eating another food. These undetected food allergies are typically masked or covered up by the body so that *the complete, intense allergic reaction does not occur as long as the person continues to expose himself to the offending food.* If the person should stop eating the food, there will be a period of uncomfortable withdrawal, followed by a normal allergic state of the body during which the person will respond dramatically to the allergenic substance. For example, if you are allergic to wheat, your body's masking of the allergy might permit you to eat it fairly often because the reaction is masked, and all you may know is that you tend to have headaches or stomach gas. If you stop eating wheat for a period of time and then try eating it again, you might react dramatically by fainting or experiencing a frightening episode of racing of the heart. In effect, the body's ability to mask the full allergic reaction has been diminished by the period of abstinence from the foodstuff.

In alcoholism, then, the hypothesis is that masking prevents alcoholics from experiencing the more dramatic symptoms of allergy in response to the cereal grains, grapes, and other fruits from which the beverages are made and to which they may be sensitive. As long as the alcoholic continues to drink frequently, the complete allergic response can be held in abeyance, and the transformed lesser symptoms of masked allergy—headache, stomach distress, blurred vision, dizziness, etc.—can be tolerated, or alleviated by medications.

Somewhat related to the masking hypothesis is the notion of the body's general adaption syndrome, the G.A.S. According to Dr. Hans Selye, the body responds to all stress in the same way, regardless of the source or nature of the stress. This response to stress, or G.A.S., is the body's attempt to meet and adapt to the challenge of stress exposure. A confrontation with an armed intruder is obviously a stressful situation, as are exposures to extreme cold, participation in competitive sports, and arguments with a difficult person. A less obvious stressor, however, is an allergen—a foodstuff or other substance to which we are sensitive.

Study of food allergies suggests that when we eat or drink an offending substance, a recognizable G.A.S. pattern takes place. First is the *alarm reaction*, during which the body responds with rapid breathing and increased heart rate as the person becomes tense; the person may feel ill, sweat, and turn pale.

The second stage is the *resistance stage*, in which the body adapts to the stress and manages it successfully; the person may begin to feel well again, and there may be no outward signs of difficulty. However, the person is expending body resources in this adaptation.

The third stage in the G.A.S. pattern is the *exhaustion stage*, in which the person's resources are exhausted in the attempt to continue the balance and feelings of well-being achieved in the resistance stage. In this stage, we feel very sick.

It is in the exhaustion stage that an allergy-addiction connection can be made by the person. If the person eats or drinks more of the offending substance, then he may restore the conditions of the resistance stage; he will once again temporarily adapt to the stress of the allergen and feel good. In effect, the G.A.S. theory of allergy and addiction is very much like the "hair of the dog that bit you" business that alcoholics joke about. If a lot of an alcoholic beverage the night before has made us feel very sick, then a bit of the same stuff the next morning is one quick way to feel better. Unfortunately, what we don't realize is that quick cures for what may be an "allergic hang-over" to the cereal grains, grapes, and fruit of alcoholic beverages are not cures at all, but invitations to a vicious cycle that no amount of drinking will help.

Not all scientists and medical practitioners would endorse the views of the clinical ecologists on allergy and addiction. Many are openly scornful of the role that allergy may play in mental, emotional, and behavioral problems in general. Hence, it is not surprising that their skepticism would extend to alcoholism as well. While skepticism about any theory of alcoholism, including allergy, is healthy, a closed mind is not. At this stage in our understanding, we should remain open to all reasonable possibilities, rejecting only those that promise more harm than good to alcoholics and those that experience and research have invalidated thoroughly.

Allergy is just one of the suggested physical explanations of the origins of alcoholism. In subsequent pages, we will take up intriguing new findings from genetics and from the world of brain chemistry. For the moment, however, let's return to the fourfold model of alcoholism presented earlier.

While alcoholism is believed to be, in part, a physical disease of the body, it would be a mistake to overlook the critical role of psychological factors in this illness. There is no compelling scientific evidence that alcoholism is *caused* by psychological factors such as depressions, anxieties, fears, resentments, and so forth. However, these painful inner emotional states must be dealt with if recovery from alcoholism is to be achieved. Anger and resentment, for example, cannot be said to cause alcoholism. But it is doubtful that habitually angry and resentful persons will be able to stay away from alcohol, or will be happy in doing so. Anger and resentments, like many negative emotional states, can trigger drinking episodes. And once the drinking has begun, the initial reasons or excuses for picking up a drink quickly become irrelevant. A drinking episode that begins with an emotional reaction or state will be *maintained* by the alcoholic's deepening physiological need for alcohol as the drinking bout proceeds over time. In some cases, frank physical need for alcohol will appear early in a drinking bout. In other cases, the drinking can go on for longer periods (perhaps days or even weeks) before physiological need is aroused and compulsive, uncontrolled drinking becomes apparent.

Numerous psychological triggers to drinking complicate our recoveries from alcoholism, especially in the early going. In our family situations, excessive guilt over actions from our alcoholic pasts can make drinking look attractive (even though it is drinking that led to the alcoholic actions that led to guilt).

A bad case of self-pity can be a dangerous state for many alcoholics. As most veteran drinkers know, an ounce of self-pity can be transformed readily into two ounces of bourbon.

Feeling too down or too high is problematic for us, since depression and euphoria are unbalanced and even unpleasant states. Sometimes we say we need alcohol to cheer us when we are feeling low. But then we say we need it to relax!

Anxiety, fear, and lack of self-confidence are ready triggers for drinking for some alcoholics, while feelings of inferiority and low self-esteem trigger others to reach for a drink. Loneliness is sometimes an ache and at other times a terror that only a drink seems to quiet down.

Attitudes are still other psychological factors that affect our recoveries from alcoholism. If we are the kind of persons who walk around with a chip on our shoulders, we will soon be fighting, not only with other people but with alcohol as well. Anti-social attitudes in general do not mix well with recovery from alcoholism.

Pessimistic attitudes toward life can drain our resolve to stay sober. Overly optimistic attitudes may set us up for a fall when our unrealistic expectations go unfulfilled.

Social factors are the third major element in understanding alcoholism as a fourfold illness. Like most creatures, human and nonhuman, we alcoholics are influenced greatly by our social surrounds. If we live in a heavy-drinking neighborhood or town, chances are very good that we will drink heavily too. The great steel manufacturing towns of the Northeastern and Midwestern United States were famous not only for their productivity, but for their enormous per capita consumption of alcoholic beverages. The wild and crazy drinking in the frontier towns of America's westward expansion is dramatic testimony to the power of social forces to shape dangerous drinking practices.

Many of us chose or drifted into occupations in which heavy drinking was not only accepted but often rewarded. Popular musicians—rock, jazz, and country—are notorious drinkers. So are house painters, poets, and novelists. Salesmen, career soldiers and sailors, and coal miners are often heavy drinkers. Perhaps less well-known is the fact that college and university professors are too.

Through observation and imitation of others around us, we socially learn many of our drinking practices, styles, and attitudes. *If we happen to be fated for alcoholism by our genes and body chemistries, then our social surrounds can constitute the environmental match that ignites the biological gasoline.* An alcoholic in a nondrinking society would not be noticeably different from other people. In a drinking society, however, the insidious disease would be encouraged and nourished, culminating finally in the complex destructiveness of dangerous drinking.

The final dimension in this fourfold disease is spiritual. For many drinking alcoholics, life is a meaningless exercise in futility. Despite the intensity of the drunken episode, alcohol drives out meaning and ushers in a life devoid of purpose. A pervasive sense of hopelessness, sorrow, and yearning is the lot of many drinking alcoholics. These feelings of dread, of inner emptiness and despair, must give way to fulfillment, hope, wholeness, and joy. Spiritual development is the key to achieving these more positive states of mind and existence.

It is unfortunate that spirituality has been often confused with religiosity. Religion is an organized body of belief, ritual, and practices that a person must endorse and follow in order to be a member of that particular group. Spirituality, however, in its most general sense, refers to the nonmaterial nature and soul of the human being. Spirituality can be nurtured and developed in the context of organized religions of all kinds, and many alcoholics have found peace in a church of their own choosing.

But spirituality need not be found only through organized religion and conventional religious concepts. For many alcoholics, approaches other than organized religion may be the paths to the garden of the spirit.

We will talk more about these other paths farther along.

CHAPTER 4

New Light on the Disease

Among those of us who have personally experienced the suffering of alcoholism, there is little doubt that alcoholism is a disease. Our pain was simply too great and our individual sorrows too deep for us to believe otherwise.

But while we alcoholics may believe that alcoholism is, in part, a physical disease of the body, we must be prepared to accept the fact that not everybody will agree with us. Although the stigma that attends our illness is steadily decreasing as knowledge spreads throughout our communities, some people still cling to the old-fashioned ideas that we alcoholics are weak-willed, irresponsible, or morally depraved. Fortunately for us alcoholics, there have been startling breakthroughs on the physical aspects of our disease in the past decade, and scientists from various institutions of higher learning, research institutes, and major hospitals around the world are now in a heated race to unlock the mysteries of alcoholism as a disease of the body.

Much of this recent research activity has centered on the brain—its chemistry and electrical activity. After all, the primary target of alcohol and other drugs is the brain and its delicate balances of impulses, signals, and information transmissions. If the human body can be said to have a "command center," then it is surely the brain. Far more intricate than the most complex computer, the human brain consists of a vast network of com-

17

munication lines, stations, and relays. From the fifteen billion neurons or nerve cells that make up the information-processing functions of our brains, thousands of messages flash from neuron to neuron and to various parts of our bodies. These messages not only result in symphonies, novels, Olympic gold medals, and other magnificent achievements, they monitor and control the very basics of life—our heart beats, respirations, body temperatures, blood pressures, and so forth. Since the brain is a sea of chemical and electrical signaling processes, it is small wonder that potent chemicals like alcohol, marijuana, and cocaine can smash through its barriers and disrupt its delicate processes in a manner that can threaten life itself.

But what of alcoholism and addiction to drugs? Can modern study of the brain and its chemistry tell us why some of us who drink fall victim to alcoholism and others do not? Why some of us cannot leave drugs like cocaine or morphine alone?

Recently, the search for answers to these questions has centered on the brain's *neurotransmitters*, chemicals released from the neurons into the spaces that separate them from other neurons. In effect, the way that a message jumps the gap from one neuron to another is by a chemical signaling system.

The neurotransmitters are fascinating substances. Produced in the brain itself, different types of these chemicals are now thought to be involved in neurological diseases such as Parkinson's Disease and in mental illnesses such as schizophrenia and serious depression.

Some of these chemicals that the brain produces are narcotic-like substances—in effect, the brain produces its own morphine. Beta-endorphin, met-enkephalin, and leu-enkephalin are morphine-like substances produced in the brain, which have pain-killing properties similar to opiate-narcotic drugs. *One recent theory of why some people develop an addiction to heroin while others do not is that the heroin addict is either born with or develops a deficiency in the brain's supply of these natural morphine-like substances.* It is very interesting to note that these same morphine-like brain chemicals have been implicated in alcoholism as well. Some studies have shown deficiencies in beta-endorphin levels in alcoholics. Moreover, recent Russian studies have pointed to possible involvement of enkephalin deficiency in alcohol addiction. The structure of enkephalins is a sequence of five ordinary amino acids, which act in the brain much like narcotic-like substances.

The term endorphin, by the way, is a contraction of two words, "endogenous" and "morphine." Since endogenous means "inner," the term means the brain's *inner morphine.* Enkephalin is Greek for "from the head."

Not all of the brain's chemicals are morphine-like substances. One of the neurotransmitters, *serotonin,* is produced from L-tryptophan, a substance

Communication between two neurons

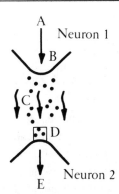

An impulse (A) travels to the end point (B) of Neuron 1 and packets of neurotransmitters (C) are spilled into the gap or synapse that separates the two neurons. The neurotransmitters bind to a specific receptor on the adjacent neuron (D), and a new impulse (E) is generated; the message travels on.

found in common foods like milk, white meat of turkey, and bananas. First discovered in 1954, serotonin attracted much interest because of its similarity to the psychedelic drug LSD.

Recently, serotonin has been implicated in alcoholism by research that shows that sharp reductions of the level of this chemical in the brain results in increases in drinking. On the other hand, increasing the availability of serotonin in the brain appears to lower the intake of alcohol in alcohol-dependent animals and humans. Serotonin is also involved in insomnia and depression.

Dopamine is another neurotransmitter of interest. It is derived from the common amino acid tyrosine. A deficiency of this chemical in the brain results in Parkinson's Disease, a neurological disorder that shows up as we age. An excess of dopamine in the brain has been associated with the mental illness schizophrenia. It is interesting to note that stimulants like amphetamine ("speed") and cocaine result in bursts of dopamine release in the brain. When the dopamine level reaches a certain extreme level, it is not uncommon for people taking large quantities of these stimulants to show a psychotic reaction that is in some ways similar to the mental illness schizophrenia. Since schizophrenia seems to be related to dopamine excess, it is not surprising that these stimulating drugs which raise dopamine levels in the brain can also result in symptoms of mental illnesses.

Still another neurotransmitter that interests scientists in the field of addictions is *noradrenaline*. Synthesized in the brain from dopamine, noradrenaline may play a role in addiction to heroin, codeine, morphine, Percodan, and other opiate-narcotic drugs since the level of this chemical is very high during narcotic withdrawal. When this high level of noradrenaline in the narcotics addict's brain is reduced by certain medications, the intense craving for the drugs can be alleviated and the person can be brought to a drug-free state. Some physicians have begun exploring the usefulness of medications that reduce noradrenaline during withdrawal from alcohol in alcoholics as well. It is entirely possible that alcoholics also have noradrenaline surges in their brains during withdrawal and that these chemical surges set up craving for more alcohol.

These neurotransmitters acting alone are of much interest in the field of alcoholism. The fact that they can combine with other substances to form further chemical products in the brain is of even greater significance. One of these other substances with which the neurotransmitters can react is *acetaldehyde*, the first breakdown product of alcohol in the body.

When we drink alcohol, certain enzymes in our bodies go to work on the alcohol and change it to acetaldehyde. Acetaldehyde is actually more poisonous than alcohol. Our bodies want to get rid of it as fast as possible — and usually do so — because if the acetaldehyde is left to build up in our systems, we will become very sick. (This is how the medication *Antabuse* works. Antabuse blocks the enzymes that normally break down the acetaldehyde to harmless substances. So if we should drink alcohol while taking Antabuse, the build-up of acetaldehyde in our bodies would make us sick.)

But, to return to the main point, when we drink alcohol, our bodies first change it to acetaldehyde. The acetaldehyde reacts chemically with the neurotransmitters to make products called TIQs. The letters TIQ are a simplification for the family of brain chemicals called tetrahydroisoquinolines. Different TIQs are formed by acetaldehyde (and other aldehydes) reacting with the various transmitters. For example, when dopamine reacts with acetaldehyde, a new substance called *salsolinol* is formed. Thus, salsolinol is a TIQ that can be formed in our brains when we drink alcohol. When serotonin condenses with aldehydes, substances called beta-carbolines are formed.

The fascinating thing about these TIQs is that when they are infused into the brains of monkeys, the monkeys develop a liking for alcohol that is quite remarkable. In the wild, monkeys do not normally prefer alcohol over water; in fact, they avoid alcohol altogether. But in Dr. R. D. Myers' laboratories at the University of North Carolina in Chapel Hill, monkeys treated with TIQs not only prefer alcohol to water, they drink enormous quantities — in some cases, the human equivalent of two quarts of 80-proof liquor a day!

A quick guide to neurotransmitters

Neurotransmitter	Source	Function	Effect on drinking/drug-taking
Dopamine	Synthesized from the amino acid L-tyrosine	Involved in Parkinson's Disease, schizophrenia	Released into brain by cocaine and amphetamines; high levels as a result of drug-taking may cause a cocaine or amphetamine psychosis.
Noradrenaline	Synthesized from dopamine	Involved in narcotic addiction and withdrawal, alcohol withdrawal, panic states	High levels occur during narcotic withdrawal and possibly during alcohol withdrawal; high levels seem to be involved in panic and anxiety states.
Serotonin	Synthesized from the amino acid L-tryptophan	Involved in depression, insomnia, and alcoholism	Low levels in brain are associated with excessive drinking; higher levels with reductions in excessive drinking.
GABA	An amino acid found in bacteria, yeast, and green plants. In brain it is synthesized from glutamic acid.	The brain's major inhibitory transmitter; inhibits impulse transmission in brain	Low levels in brain due to excessive drinking can result in alcoholic convulsions. GABA system is potentiated by Valium and Librium.
B-endorphin Met-enkephalin Leu-enkephalin	Pituitary hormone beta-lipotropin, other brain locations	Natural brain narcotic-like substances that reduce pain	Deficiencies may be involved in alcoholism or narcotic addiction.

While some scientists continue to disbelieve this line of research on TIQs, others regard it as a major breakthrough in understanding the origins of alcoholism. There are several points here that even the harshest critics of the disease concept of alcoholism must acknowledge.

First, these animals who do not normally prefer alcohol over water develop a striking alcohol habit once their brains are treated with TIQs. Second, TIQs are actually formed in the brain and are products of alcohol drinking. Third, when alcoholics come into treatment centers, they show elevated levels of TIQs. Fourth, while animals can be trained by other methods to prefer weak solutions of alcohol over water, the concentrations of alcohol reach very high levels in the TIQ research (80-proof). Finally, once TIQs have been infused and a stable drinking pattern established, the animal's high level of alcohol consumption appears to be *irreversible*. The TIQ-treated animal drinks and drinks and drinks — much like his alcoholic human counterpart!

Why do TIQs appear to produce addiction to alcohol? On comparison of chemical structures, one is struck by the close similarity of certain TIQs to *morphine*. Tetrahydropapaveroline (THP) is a type of TIQ formed when the transmitter dopamine condenses with the aldehyde called dopaldehyde. We now know that THP binds to the same sites in the brain that beta-endorphin and morphine do. In effect, many of these TIQs and beta-carbolines are not only products of alcohol drinking, they look and act very much like narcotic-like substances in the brain. Our brains have played a cruel joke on us. *What may have gone in our mouths as a martini or a beer ends up in the biochemical machinery of the brain as a compound very similar to the highly addictive substance morphine or its natural twin, beta-endorphin.*

As we mentioned previously, narcotics addicts may be people who either are born with or have developed a deficiency in beta-endorphin, the brain's own natural morphine-like substance. Alcoholics also may have an inborn or a developed deficiency in beta-endorphin. Since the body is able to piece together its own beta-endorphin or morphine-like substances (the TIQs) from alcohol, we alcoholics may be unable to stop drinking once we start because drinking itself provides the morphine-like substances missing in our brain chemistry.

Not all scientists would agree that TIQs, serotonin, beta-carbolines, or any other neurochemicals are the underlying physical causes of addicted drinking. But many scientists are convinced that the answers are surely here in the chemistry of the brains of alcoholics: if not these particular brain chemicals, then some other neurochemical acting in similar fashion will ultimately unlock the mystery of this disease.

How the addictive products TIQs and beta-carbolines are formed in the body

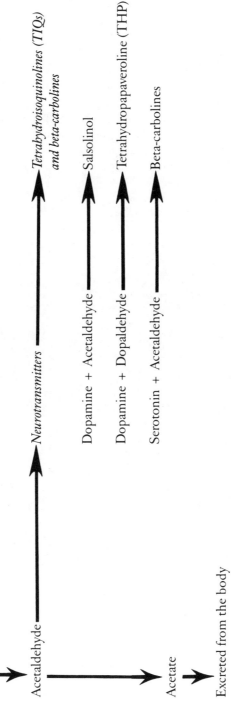

Alcohol

Acetaldehyde → Neurotransmitters → *Tetrahydroisoquinolines (TIQs) and beta-carbolines*

Dopamine + Acetaldehyde → Salsolinol

Dopamine + Dopaldehyde → Tetrahydropapaveroline (THP)

Serotonin + Acetaldehyde → Beta-carbolines

Acetate

Excreted from the body

Alcohol is metabolized to acetaldehyde. Acetaldehyde and other aldehydes condense with neurotransmitters to produce tetrahydroisoquinolines (TIQs) and beta-carbolines. These compounds, formed when we drink alcohol, appear to be highly addictive brain substances similar to morphine precursors. Infused into animal brains, they produce what seems to be irreversible addictive drinking.

Until scientists uncover the precise nature of these complex chemical processes in our brains, the lesson is clear. We alcoholics cannot instruct our brains not to produce TIQs when we drink. We cannot use willpower to change our brain levels of dopamine, serotonin, and noradrenaline during a night out on the town drinking heavily. And no amount of wishing it were otherwise will correct the fundamental errors in our neurochemistry and physiology that complicate our drinking.

We alcoholics cannot exercise *consistent* control over our drinking and our behavior while drinking. The reason we cannot exercise consistent control is in our *brains* and not "all in our minds."

CHAPTER 5

Other Problems

Alcoholism is a primary disease in its own right. It is not a symptom of an underlying psychiatric disorder. But having said this, we need also to recognize that while alcoholism is not a symptom of something else, *alcoholics* can develop more than one illness or problem. Alcoholics are human beings, and like all human beings they can fall victim to other serious physical and mental illnesses. These other problems are often overlooked in alcoholics, but it is best to discuss them openly and honestly.

Severe depression is a problem for some alcoholics that may require professional diagnosis and treatment. In general, there are two major types of depression. One of these types is called *exogenous depression* and refers to depressions we all experience at some time or another. Exogenous means "outer." Hence, an exogenous depression is one that occurs in response to a situation outside ourselves. It is also called a *reactive depression* in that the person reacts to a situation with depression. Death of a loved one, loss of an important job, divorce, a serious financial reversal, and a major deception by a significant person in our lives are examples of the types of events that can trigger an exogenous depression. This type of depression has an identifiable situational cause and a clear starting point. A person can usually determine when the depression started and what probably caused it. Depending on severity, this type of depression may pass without treatment. It may respond favorably to renewed commitment to one's program of recovery from alcoholism or it may require professional counseling or psychotherapy. Recovering alcoholics often go in and out of these reactive depressions, especially in the early periods of recovery. Alcoholics suffering from temporary, reactive depressions do not require medications and, as a rule, should not be treated with these.

The second type of depression, *endogenous depression*, affects far fewer alcoholics. The word endogenous means "inner." Hence, an endogenous depression is one that is caused by inner, biological factors rather than outer, environmental happenings. Endogenous depressions are thought to be related to deficiencies in particular brain neurotransmitters (see Chapter 4). Two brain chemicals, *serotonin* and *noradrenaline*, may be involved. Serotonin is sometimes referred to as the "molecule of depression," and as we grow older, levels of this particular neurotransmitter may fall. When serotonin levels in the brain are low, depression and insomnia are thought to take place.

Medications called antidepressants are used to combat biological depressions. Antidepressants should not be thought of as tranquilizers like Valium or Librium. The pharmacology of antidepressants is in no way similar to tranquilizers, and alcoholics who have to take antidepressants on physicians' orders should not feel guilty about doing so. For the most part, antidepressants seem to work by restoring the availability of either serotonin or noradrenaline in the brain.

It is not always easy for experts to tell which type of depression a person has, biological or reactive. Laboratory tests are available, and they may be more or less useful depending on the results and the skill of the physician in interpreting findings. A physician may test for serotonin or noradrenaline levels in the brain by using tests that measure metabolic byproducts of these neurotransmitters in body fluids such as urine and spinal fluid. The trouble is that these metabolic byproduct measurements on body fluids don't always accurately reflect what is happening to the neurotransmitters in the brain itself.

Physicians may also wish to do special tests for thyroid function since studies have shown that as many as ten percent of the cases of depression may be due to lowered thyroid function. Care must be taken here, however, because the routine thyroid tests that are commonly ordered by physicians are not sensitive enough to detect this type of hypothyroidism. If serious depression is an issue, the physician may order a test called a TRH stimulation test. In the TRH test, the body's thyroid stimulating hormone (TSH) is measured in response to injections of thyrotropin releasing hormone (TRH). An augmented TSH response to such injections indicates hypothyroidism which, in turn, *may* be a factor in a biological depression. If there is evidence of low thyroid function, the physician may want to treat it with thyroid hormone.

Still another test that may help the physician to determine whether or not a depression is biological or situational is the Dexamethasone Suppression Test or DST. This test concerns the body's *endocrine* glands – in particular, the pituitary and adrenal glands. Both the pituitary and the adrenals are involved in the body's production of *corticosteroids*, hormones that control key processes in the body. In the DST test, the physician watches what happens to the body's production of *cortisol* when dexamethasone is administered over a period of time. Cortisol is a particular steroid whose level is controlled by pituitary secretions which are, in turn, controlled by the adrenal glands. Dexamethasone is a potent synthetic steroid that usually suppresses secretion from the pituitary gland. If the pituitary secretion of cortisol is *not* suppressed by the dexamethasone, then a biological depression may be suspected.

In considering specialized tests for depression, alcoholics should remember one important fact: *these tests are not reliable with intoxicated people, nor are they reliable in the early period of abstinence from alcohol.* At least a month or so of sobriety should be in place before a test like the DST is done.

Another problem that some alcoholics may show is *manic-depressive* illness, in which the person's moods swing radically and regularly from high to low. The manic-depressive is excitable, talkative, and given to rapid movements, thinking, and talk. Judgment is often poor and impulsive actions are typical. For alcoholics who suffer from this additional serious illness, treatment with a mineral, lithium, is often helpful. Lithium treatment is a complex therapy that should always be in the hands of a well-trained physician. There are troublesome side effects of lithium treatment and regular blood testing is a necessity.

Some alcoholics may develop serious mental illnesses grouped together under the label of *schizophrenia*. Like the other biological illnesses we have been discussing, schizophrenic illnesses are related to the brain's chemistry. In certain cases, treatment by a physician with medications called phenothiazines may be necessary. Thorazine is perhaps the most well-known medication of this type. These antischizophrenic medications should not be confused with tranquilizers like Valium or Librium, since their action in the brain is quite different. Phenothiazines act to reduce brain levels of the neurotransmitter *dopamine*, which are often elevated in persons suffering from schizophrenia. Instead of prescribing phenothiazines, physicians may choose to prescribe *Haldol* for these conditions. Unfortunately, all antischizophrenic medications have serious side effects, some of which grow worse over time.

Alcoholics who have to take medications like thyroid hormone, lithium, tricyclic antidepressants, Haldol, or phenothiazines because of serious illnesses in addition to their alcoholism should not feel guilty for taking these necessary medications. And they should not be made to feel guilty by other alcoholics who may misunderstand these medications and their purposes. Alcoholics with serious mental illnesses have not slipped or relapsed when they take medications as ordered by well-trained and knowledgeable physicians. Psychoactive medications are not all alike, and they cannot be thought of simplistically as "pills," or "dry booze," or "tranquilizers."

As modern science is now showing, certain mental illnesses are biological diseases heavily influenced by heredity. In manic-depressive illness, for example, we now believe that a greater than normal number of certain brain *receptors* is somehow related to the genetic factor in this disease. What are these receptors that seem to be the basis for the heredity factor in serious, biological depression?

In Chapter 4, we saw that the brain is a sea of many chemicals. Some of these chemicals, neurotransmitters, form the basis for the brain's communication system. Messages that travel from one nerve cell (neuron) to another do so via these chemical transmitters. When an impulse reaches the end of one nerve cell, tiny packets of chemicals (neurotransmitters) are released into the gap that separates one nerve cell from another. These chemicals bind to specific *receptors* on the surface of the adjacent nerve cell. When the level of the chemical reaches a sufficient amount in the receptor on the adjacent nerve cell, a new impulse is triggered in this second cell and the message travels on. In this way, a message may reach several thousand neurons. Everything that human beings do depends upon this basic, simple communication process involving neurons, neurotransmitters, and receptors. This is how the brain maintains vital human functions like breathing, pulse rate, blood pressure, and body temperature control. It is also how the brain conceives symphonies, novels, lofty philosophical thoughts, and poetry. Neurotransmitters enable us to play baseball, win at tennis, make love, and read this book.

The brain does have other methods of internal communication. It is possible, for example, that direct communication from one neuron to another can happen without the use of neurotransmitters. With regard to both mental illness and the addictions, however, brain neurotransmitter systems have been the major focus of research.

As we saw in Chapter 4, addictions like alcoholism and various forms of drug addiction are now thought to involve excesses or deficiencies of various neurotransmitters like serotonin, beta-endorphin, noradrenaline, dopamine, and also reactions of these transmitters with other chemicals in the body.

In manic-depressive illnesses, however, recent research is suggesting that the disease is linked to problems with the *receptors*, and not to excesses or deficiencies of the specific transmitter chemicals. What seems to be happening in manic-depressive illness is that there is an abundance of particular receptors called *muscarinic cholinergic receptors.*

In effect, an alcoholic who has the extra burden of manic-depressive illness is the victim of not one hereditary biological disease, but two. He suffers from alcoholism and manic-depressive illness. Since both illnesses can be arrested but not cured, the manic-depressive alcoholic may be able to work a program of recovery like Alcoholics Anonymous, but he will need professional care as well. In all probability he will have to take medication under the care of a physician for the rest of his life.

Phobias, anxiety, and panic attacks are a second major class of other problems that recovering alcoholics may develop. For years it was assumed that these unpleasant experiences were merely symptoms of "poor adjustment," "neurotic character," or "emotional disturbance." Modern scientific thinking, however, has turned to both *behavioral learning theory* and *neurobiology* to explain these nagging and persistent human problems.

Phobias are unreasonable fears of some specific object, person, event, animal, or situation. While the feared object is known to the sufferer, the origin of the fear is not known. The person does not know why he has the fear or how it originated. He may acknowledge its crippling effects but be powerless to do anything about it. People have shown phobias to an amazing collection of objects — from high winds to the man in the moon! Fear of dogs, furry animals, high places, open spaces, enclosed rooms, hot weather, cold weather, school, and snakes are common.

For the most part, phobias are *learned* fears. They may start early in life when an unpleasant happening gets paired up with some previously innocuous object. For example, a bad early experience with a vicious dog may be forgotten, but the fear of dogs remains. These specific fears in alcoholics may respond favorably to a form of behavioral therapy called *systematic desensitization therapy.* Usually administered by a trained psychologist, this form of therapy allows the person to imagine parts of the feared situation or object while in a relaxed state. Eventually, the person imagines the complete feared object or situation without fear. A final test in the actual situation or with the object is done to assess actual change in fear.

Phobias are learned responses to specific things, while anxiety is a more diffuse and generalized state. The anxious person seems to "carry his anxiety with him" from situation to situation. Recent thought about anxiety has moved away from a strictly learned explanation of this uncomfortable state to a recognition of a number of underlying biological factors. Many substances are now known to produce the experience of intense anxiety when given to human subjects. Dr. Alessandro Guidotti at the National Institute of Mental Health Laboratory of Preclinical Pharmacology showed that a substance produced by the body, called DBI, heightens anxiety. It is curious to note that DBI attaches to the same receptors that Valium does, but instead of calming the person down, DBI makes the person anxious.

Another group of substances, the beta-carbolines, has been shown to cause extreme anxiety. Claus Braestrup, a Danish researcher, gave beta-carbolines to patient volunteers and provoked extreme anxiety attacks in them. Drs. Phil Skolnick and Steven Paul injected monkeys with beta-carbolines and observed almost immediate physical signs of extreme anxiety: rapid pulse rate and elevated blood pressure, failure to eat and drink, distress sounds, marked turning of the head and body, and so forth. Hormonal changes and neurotransmitter changes consistent with high anxiety occurred as well. These results with beta-carbolines are very interesting because alcohol researchers are now discovering that certain beta-carbolines infused into the brains of animals produce heavy drinking of alcohol. It is possible that the preference for alcohol over water by these animals is due to the biological arousal of heavy anxiety by these beta-carbolines; the animals may be using the alcohol to reduce their anxiety.

Dr. Merton Sandler of Queen Charlotte's Maternity Hospital in London has found in urine an unidentified chemical which is suppressed by Valium and alcohol. Dr. Sandler proposed that some alcoholics may drink compulsively in order to deal with an overabundance of this anxiety-provoking chemical. Still other body chemicals—one called Ro 15-1788, for instance—are capable of neutralizing the actions of tranquilizers like Valium or Librium.

Some new theories focus on the heart as well as on areas of the brain. A heart condition called mitral valve prolapse is believed by some specialists to be an underlying reason for some attacks of extreme anxiety. The heart's mitral valve, situated between the left atrium and the left ventricle, normally allows blood to flow into the ventricle. In mitral valve prolapse, the valve is defective and does not close properly. As a result, blood can leak backwards into the atrium. A number of unpleasant symptoms can be associated with this condition: fatigue due to reduced output of the heart, shortness of breath, episodes of racing heartbeat, anxiety, and panic attacks. In some cases, treatment of the heart condition, with cardiac medications like Inderal or other drugs called beta blockers, has the added benefit of helping to ease crippling anxiety and panic attacks.

Scientists interested in understanding the causes of crippling fear, anxiety, and panic have made great advances in recent years. We now know that a neurotransmitter called GABA (gamma aminobutyric acid) is very much involved with how tranquilizers work in the brain. GABA is an abundant transmitter found throughout the brain and spinal cord. It plays an inhibitory role in the central nervous system. A tranquilizer like Valium seems to work by facilitating the actions of GABA in our brains. It should be noted that GABA is not a foreign chemical or drug, but a natural chemical produced in the brain itself. People with anxiety disorders may suffer from deficiencies of some kind or another in the GABA system. It is also interesting to note that excessive alcohol consumption over a period of time interferes with the GABA system. When GABA function has been seriously disturbed by drinking, extreme anxiety and convulsions are more likely to occur when we try to stop our intake of alcohol. *In short, certain of the symptoms we have during withdrawal from alcohol—agitation, fear, extreme anxiety, and convulsions—are probably caused directly by the effects of heavy drinking on GABA.*

Certain other alcohol withdrawal symptoms that bear upon anxiety, fear, and panic may involve the neurotransmitter *noradrenaline*. In both heroin and alcohol withdrawal, the brain of the addict and the alcoholic is flooded by high levels of noradrenaline. The *locus ceruleus*, a small blue spot in the brain, is hyperactive during heroin and alcohol withdrawal. Since the locus ceruleus synthesizes most of the noradrenaline in the brain, its hyperactivity results in surges of this particular neurotransmitter. High levels of noradrenaline have striking effects on blood pressure, sending it skyrocketing to very high levels. The chemical can also trigger off various rhythmic disturbances in the heart. In effect, when the brain is flooded with noradrenaline, the person experiences anxiety. Medications used to reduce blood pressure in nonalcoholics and non-heroin-addicted patients with high blood pressure have been found to be effective in heroin addicts and alcoholics by Drs. Mark Gold, Carter Pottash, and H. D. Kleber. *Clonidine*, a drug used to combat hypertension, has been shown to be effective in both heroin and alcohol withdrawal. Clonidine's effectiveness is due to its ability to reduce noradrenaline levels in the brain.

Dr. D. E. Redmond has suggested that a new theory of anxiety may be built upon locus ceruleus hyperactivity. Also, there is now reason to believe that noradrenaline surges from this small brain structure may play a role in cardiovascular stress and cardiac-related anxiety symptoms. Some recovering alcoholics may continue to show unpleasant anxiety and stress symptoms long after formal detoxification is over. For this unfortunate group of recovering persons, locus ceruleus hyperactivity and noradrenaline "storms" in the brain may not end when withdrawal is over, but may continue well on into recovery.

This modern research on fear, anxiety, and panic states is of great importance to recovering alcoholics. While many alcoholics are able to achieve a comfortable sobriety through personal growth programs alone, others seem to have enormous difficulty in achieving states of balance, serenity, and freedom from fear and anxiety. As research sheds more light on the heart and the cardiovascular system and their relationship to anxiety states, more alcoholics may come to know some peace in their lives. If a particular recovering alcoholic understands that his constant anxiety may be due to a defective valve in his heart and not to a particular defect of personal adjustment, that knowledge may provide renewed hope for recovery, while medical treatments are tested and proved effective and safe. Similarly, as the role of the chemistry of the brain in anxiety, fear, and panic is further clarified and understood, recovering alcoholics with crippling disorders may find new and helpful advances in treatment available to them. *Recovering alcoholics cannot solve their fear and anxiety problems through use of tranquilizers like Valium or Librium. Not only are these tranquilizers ineffective in treating certain fear reactions, they are dangerous because they are likely to lead to a second addiction.*

Panic attacks, a truly crippling and debilitating anxiety reaction, will not respond to tranquilizers or other sedatives. These attacks can be treated very effectively, however, with minute doses of imipramine, a nontranquilizer and nonaddictive substance that is an antidepressant. It is believed that anti-depressants of two types—tricyclics and monoamine oxidase inhibitors—can reduce panic attacks because of their ability to inhibit the locus ceruleus. Common sense would not lead one to suppose that antidepressant medications would cause panic attacks to cease. Only scientific understanding of the brain and its chemistry could lead us to this important breakthrough that involves medications other than the tranquilizers which have been so dangerous to alcoholics.

Many recovering alcoholics go through periods when the obsessive energies they once focussed on drinking get attached to some person, place, or thing. These *other obsessions* in sobriety are not only extraordinarily painful, but they can virtually cripple alcoholics and drive them dangerously close to drinking and relapse.

In some cases, the recovering person gets fixated on another person, and an intense love affair ensues. These often stormy, obsessional relationships masquerade as love, but they rarely have much in common with the respect, caring, and positive growth that can take place in a mature, adult relationship. Obsessional relationships usually evolve when two dependent people cling to each other—making each other's life miserable through insecurity, jealousy, fighting, constant physical closeness with no real intimacy, and an inability to end the relationship or make it better.

A positive love relationship involves freedom-giving rather than enslavement, respect and caring, genuine intimacy, mutual need satisfaction, and interdependence rather than dependence. Interdependent relationships involve two strong, independent people who come together out of choice to enhance each other's growth. The key word here is choice. Love is not only possible in these mature relationships, but very probable.

Compulsive relationships, on the other hand, begin with both partners' egotistical needs being met. Each person takes from the relationship an idealized image of themselves. They "love" their partners because their partners let them see themselves as they want to see themselves. Although neither partner realizes it or says it, the following is taking place: "I love you, not because of you, but because of how you make *me* feel and think about *myself." In effect, in obsessional love relationships the person usually falls in love with himself or herself.* When the attraction to the other person is no longer strong enough for this bit of narcissistic mirroring to go on, the person begins to hate the other for no longer making him feel good and able to think positively about himself. Now the unrecognized and unexpressed thoughts are as follows: "You used to make me feel good and love myself, but now you make me feel bad and hate myself. Therefore, I hate you since hating me is unacceptable."

These other obsessions in recovering alcoholics are intense, painful, and difficult to change. They may involve children, gambling, particular sexual acts, careers and jobs, authority and control over others, material possessions like houses and properties, and so forth. Regardless of the nature of these other obsessions, recovering alcoholics must try to see the reality of them as they did with their earlier obsessions with alcohol. Looking carefully at the consequences of these obsessions and seeing how they hurt us rather than help us is of value. Gaining insight into what is really going on in an obsessional relationship may also help us to change it or release it. Working a Twelve Steps program on these additional obsessions is clearly helpful. Admitting that we are powerless over another person, gambling, a job, and so forth may help us, just as such surrender helped with our alcoholic obsession. Turning the obsession over to our higher powers and doing an inventory on it are also useful. For some recovering persons, however, professional help with these problems may be essential if the obsession is to be overcome and some peace achieved.

Any discussion of mental and emotional difficulties that may trouble us in recovery would not be complete without mentioning *anger*. Many recovering people never learned to deal with anger. Many of us either passively accept everything that comes our way or we explode suddenly into unpredictable rages and tantrums. We don't get angry when we really should, and then we blow up like volcanoes over some trivial happening.

Part of our difficulty with anger is simply that we never learned a good solid repertoire of anger responses. Our "anger systems" involve little more than "on-off switches." We shut up. We explode. We keep our feelings under tight control. We blow up.

We need to know how to tell an aggressive, loud, and offensive person to go away, instead of suffering their poor manners in silence or suddenly screaming back at them. We need mild warning signals to let other people know they are about to go too far and had better back off. And we need tactics short of full-blown attacks to get troublesome coworkers off our cases or to get our bosses to admit we may have a point. *In short, we recovering alcoholics need to learn a whole lot of assertive responses that vary in strength and can be used to keep situations from escalating into major confrontations.* We need to be able to discharge our anger at low levels of intensity, so that continued "stuffing" of it doesn't culminate in abrupt and explosive loss of control. Once again, some of us will need professional help to learn how to deal with our anger and how to convert it to positive, assertive actions in our own behavior.

These other problems we have discussed in this chapter are not a necessary part of alcoholism. They will affect some alcoholics, but certainly not all. Many alcoholics will enjoy a sound and satisfying recovery from alcoholism without having to cope with a serious, debilitating mental illness. Others, however, will not be so lucky. We should show great compassion and acceptance for those recovering alcoholics who must deal with further problems once sobriety has been achieved. Above all else, we should understand that our own recoveries cannot dictate the recoveries of other people, who may suffer from additional problems. As AA members are quick to affirm: *"There but for the grace of God go I."*

CHAPTER 6

A Family Disease

Given the scientific advances of the past two decades, there can be no doubt about it: alcoholism is a disease that runs in families. We can demonstrate this easily to ourselves if we have access to a large group of recovering alcoholics. When we ask those who had an alcoholic mother, father, or grandparent to raise their hands, what we see is remarkable. Roughly 80 to 90 percent of our audience will raise their hands. While this sort of evidence is impressive, it does not *prove* that heredity plays a role in alcoholism. What is needed are controlled studies that allow one to rule out the effects of different environments. Fortunately, such studies have been done and the results are now available.

In the early 1970s, Dr. Donald Goodwin and his associates reported on data gathered in Denmark. Dr. Goodwin compared the rates of alcoholism among adults who had been adopted as children. If the biological father was an alcoholic, the adopted son had a threefold increase in the risk of developing the disease. Since these children had been raised not by their biological parents but by adopted parents, the effects of being raised in an alcoholic home could not have caused this increased risk. Moreover, the rates of adult alcoholism were not increased for the adopted-out sons of non-alcoholics. Therefore, possible stress of adoption could not have caused an increase in later alcoholism.

In another study, Dr. Goodwin looked at brothers of these adoptees whose biological parents were alcoholics. These brothers had not been adopted but remained with their biological parents. If being raised in the parental alcoholic environments was a significant factor, then these brothers who were raised in their alcoholic parents' homes would have even higher rates of alcoholism in adulthood. Surprisingly, exposure to alcoholism in the primary family had no discernible effect. The rates for adult alcoholism were equally elevated in boys who had alcoholic biological parents but had been raised in adopted-out homes and boys who had been raised by their own alcoholic parents. *In effect, the increased susceptibility to alcoholism in these studies by Dr. Goodwin and coworkers was due entirely to genetics; environment played no significant role.*

Of course, one study does not tell the whole story. We cannot dismiss the possible role of differing environments on alcoholism from Goodwin's data alone. Environment may have a role in some types of alcoholism and not in others. Recent studies on Swedish adoptees by Dr. Robert Cloninger and his coworkers not only confirm Dr. Goodwin's results on genetics, but provide further information on environment acting with genetics.

Reporting on recent evidence from an ongoing study called the Stockholm Adoption Study, Dr. Cloninger pointed out two types of alcoholism. In one of these types, inheritance alone determines susceptibility to the disease. This type of alcoholism may be referred to as "environmentally independent." In the second type, inheritance must be present, but there needs to be environmental provocation for the disease to appear. This type of alcoholism is called "environmentally limited." It is usually mild and does not require treatment. In fact, this pattern more closely resembles occasional "problem drinking" than it does alcoholism.

Dr. Cloninger's findings on adopted-out children revealed an even more striking role of genetics than did Dr. Goodwin's. In the Cloninger study, if the biological fathers were alcoholics, the sons had a nine times greater risk of developing alcoholism. For daughters of female alcoholics, the risk was three times greater. As with other genetic studies, this work by Dr. Cloninger focused on children who had not been raised by their biological parents but had been placed in adoptive homes very early in their lives. In effect, these children showed the first type of alcoholism, "environmentally independent" alcoholism. Since they did not know their parents and were not raised by them, these male children in adulthood developed the type of alcoholism that was strongly linked to genetics and not at all to environment. Dr. Cloninger estimated heritability at 90 percent in these men.

For the "environmentally limited" type of problem drinking, heredity and environment teamed up to produce a twofold increase in risk for this milder and more common type of susceptibility. (It is interesting to note that a provocative environment alone, without a genetic history, resulted in an even *lower* susceptibility to alcoholism. This finding, of course, opposes the common-sense notion that environment causes alcoholism. But as science often shows, common sense is often wrong.) These studies by Goodwin in Denmark and Cloninger in Sweden agree that genetics plays a major role in the family transmission of alcoholism. *As a rule, families do not cause alcoholism and are not to blame for its appearance in a family member.* Alcoholism runs in families because of our genes, not because of what we may or may not do to each other as members of families.

To point out the very significant part that genetics plays in the origins of alcoholism does not minimize the importance of the family in the recovery process. Families suffer terribly from alcoholism in a member. Spouses may find their very identities threatened by alcoholism in a wife or husband. Children from alcoholic homes may show adjustment patterns that persist into adulthood. Parents of alcoholics may come to know profound sorrow and despair. This suffering of family members must be recognized, acknowledged, and alleviated regardless of what the ultimate fate of the alcoholic may be.

While families do not cause alcoholism in a member, they may unwittingly help to continue it. Spouses and older children may cover up for the alcoholic, minimize or excuse the drinking, and ignore its consequences. They may overlook behavior that is completely unacceptable, give up their own rights, and allow themselves to be intimidated. Without realizing that it is happening, family members may become *enablers* of the drinking.

Study of the wives of alcoholics indicated that spouses of alcoholics use a variety of coping styles, some of which may serve to continue the drinking rather than to help curb it. These coping styles are as follows:

1. *Withdrawal within the marriage.* (Shown by avoidance of the husband, sexual withdrawal, denial of spouse's own feelings, refusal to communicate.)

2. *Protection of the alcoholic.* (Pouring out liquor, explaining husband's behavior to employers, making excuses, making sure he eats.)

3. *Attack.* (Verbal abuse, locking husband out of the house, initiating discussion of divorce.)

4. *Safeguarding family interests.* (Controlling the money, keeping children away from him, paying the bills, giving him money in small amounts.)

5. *Acting out.* (Threatening suicide, getting drunk along with the alcoholic, provoking jealousy.)

Of these particular coping styles, withdrawal in marriage as shown by sexual withdrawal, refusal to communicate, avoidance of husband, and discussing termination of the marriage was shown in one study to be related to continued destructive drinking in the alcoholic. These studies on the coping styles of wives must not be taken to mean that alcoholism in husbands is *caused* by their wives' behavior. They do show, however, that certain responses of family members to alcoholism in their midst can complicate things further rather than helping.

There are some very simple rules each of us can follow if we are in any sort of relationship to the alcoholic and wish to avoid making matters worse. These rules will help if we are friend, business associate, parent, spouse, brother, sister, or fellow alcoholic trying to help another sufferer.

First, we must not allow ourselves to be misled by the alcoholic's excuses. Many alcoholics are masterful at persuading themselves and others that their drinking is reasonable and even, perhaps, deserved. At times the excuses may have what appear to be strong bases in reality. A tragic accident may have cut short a promising career in athletics, music, or the theater, leaving the alcoholic bitter and resentful. Health may fail. Old age may usher in its share of heartaches. In all of these matters, however, we must constantly keep in mind rule number one: *although there are many excuses, there is never a valid reason for an alcoholic to take a drink*.

The second rule is to keep firmly in mind the fact that we are not to blame for the alcoholic's drinking. Some alcoholics are quite capable of shifting the responsibility for their drinking to other people. If we are in close relationships to the alcoholic, chances are good that he or she will blame us. The accusations can be numerous. According to the alcoholic, we are at fault for the drinking because we make his or her life miserable, we do not give enough love, we are bad spouses, poor lovers, awful parents, insensitive persons, terrible providers, and so on and so forth. Rule number two is simply that we don't buy into these usually unwarranted attacks on our characters and personalities. It is often the case that alcoholics think so poorly of themselves that they *project* these negative and undesirable characteristics onto others. *We must not accept these accusations of blame since we are not the cause of the alcoholic's drinking.* While most of us have things about ourselves that we have to work at long and hard, we must not mix these things up with the reasons why alcoholics drink. And while we are not to blame for the drinking of alcoholics, it is important to remember that the alcoholic is also not to blame. Alcoholism is a genetically influenced disease involving the chemistry of the addict's brain. It is not a matter of willpower or choice. Rather than blame ourselves or blame alcoholics, we must help them to realize the nature of their disease and what they must do to recover. But in the final analysis, alcoholics must learn to care for themselves. While they are not responsible for developing the disease, they must take the responsibility for doing something about it.

The third rule concerns the tendency of most alcoholics to deny their alcoholism and its consequences. It is important that we who in some way or another interact with alcoholics refuse to go along with this learned tactic. Denial of the drinking, the disease, and what must be done about it are coping strategies the alcoholic has learned in response to the deepening disease process within him. Denial does serve important purposes. On the one hand, it bolsters up the alcoholic's crumbling self-esteem system which is falling apart from the terrible results of the disease. On the other hand, however, denial permits the alcoholic to do what he is compelled to do — continue the drinking at all costs. In refusing to accept the alcoholic's denial, we must be careful because we do want the drinking to stop, but we don't want to shatter completely the self-esteem of the alcoholic in the attempt. In fact, if we threaten further the alcoholic's self-esteem system, we may achieve the opposite of what we wish to happen. Many alcoholics automatically reach for a drink when their self-esteem drops below a certain point. They do the same in response to guilt, fear, anger, depression, resentment, and anxiety. Therefore, how we go about living up to rule number three is a lot more complicated than it might appear. *While we must be firm in refusing to accept the alcoholic's denial, we must also be caring, sensitive, and alert for small victories over a period of time.* Modest expectations and a firm but loving approach to alcoholics is almost always more appropriate and effective than hostile confrontations, bitter arguments, and outright attacks.

Rule number four involves recognition and acceptance of the fact that no person working alone can expect to turn active alcoholics around. From hospitalization for detoxification and rehabilitation to aftercare counseling and Alcoholics Anonymous, help in some form or another is not only available but usually necessary. *The belief that we alone can get alcoholics sober and keep them that way is irrational.* When we find ourselves thinking along these lines, we should stop and examine our own needs. Wives cannot get their husbands sober and cannot keep them sober. Children cannot get their parents sober, and parents cannot get their children sober. Friends are important to alcoholics, but friends alone are not likely to keep alcoholics sober. For most alcoholics, help must be sought. Such help need not always be professional. Meetings of Alcoholics Anonymous are held throughout the world, and all alcoholics should be encouraged to give AA at least a try.

Issues concerned with *timing* make up rule number five. For those of us who live with or work with alcoholics, it is important to remember that *nothing meaningful can be accomplished with alcoholics when they are drinking.* Once the drinking starts, our best counsel is to wait until they are dry to try to influence them. Of course, if an alcoholic is not only drinking but in need of hospitalization, firm measures must be taken to insure that the alcoholic is placed in the hands of medical professionals. However, aside from seeing that alcoholics get medical attention when appropriate, nothing positive can be expected from confrontations of any intensity with drinking alcoholics. They either fail to live up to promises made while drinking or forget the promises altogether. If the alcoholic is given to memory blackouts, he may not only forget the promises made, but the entire conversation as well! Attempts to influence some alcoholics when they have been drinking or are intoxicated can be dangerous. In these cases, we should be wary of a belligerent response or even physical assault. Family members, friends, or other associates should not hesitate to call for police, ambulances, and other sources of outside aid if the situation warrants it. For some alcoholics who drink daily and are never sober, outside sources of aid may be essential to getting them into a treatment center that specializes in care for alcoholics.

The sixth rule is simple and straightforward: *All family members should stop and look at their own drinking and drug use.* It is often the case that alcoholism, problem-drinking, or drug use in other family members is overlooked while everybody focuses on the identified alcoholic in the family. In effect, alcoholism in a wife or child may go unnoticed in comparison with the more flamboyant drinking of the husband. Since alcoholics often marry each other and since we know that alcoholism is likely to occur in the children of alcoholic families, everybody in the family needs to examine his own drug and alcohol use carefully.

Rule number seven is the last but possibly most important suggestion. Members of Al-Anon, the program for persons whose lives are bound up with alcoholics in some way, learn to *release the alcoholic with love.* This concept of release grows out of the fact that as the alcoholic's obsession with alcohol deepens, wives, husbands, or parents often get obsessed with the alcoholic. When they are able to release the alcoholic with love, these concerned persons gain freedom from their obsession. In a sense, release is to the concerned person what surrender is to the alcoholic. Both concepts are designed to deal with obsession. We must remember that release is not rejection, indifference, or hostility. When we release the alcoholic with love, we are turning him over to others, to a higher power, or to his ultimate fate, whatever that may be. Just as the alcoholic cannot get sober through willpower alone, neither can we who love him use our willpower to control him and keep him sober.

These are the six basic rules that people living near active alcoholism can follow. Stated more concisely, they are as follows:

1. Don't allow yourself to be misled by the alcoholic's excuses, because there is no valid reason for an alcoholic to drink;

2. Do not accept the blame for the alcoholic's drinking. Alcoholism is a disease, not a problem caused by spouses, friends, children, or parents;

3. Refuse to accept the denial that often goes with the disease. Continue to point out the results of the drinking when the situation is right to do so;

4. Seek out help from others, and do not entertain the thought that you and you alone can get the alcoholic sober;

5. When the alcoholic is drinking, there isn't much to be gained from trying to increase his or her insight into the problem. Never argue with an intoxicated person. Try to influence them when they are sober;

6. Stop and look at your own drinking and drug use;

7. We need to surrender to our obsession with the alcoholic just as the alcoholic needs to surrender to his obsession with alcohol.

Living with or near active alcoholism can expose us to very grave psychological, emotional, and physical risks. This is true whether we are spouses, parents, children, or friends of alcoholics. The intoxicated actions, beliefs, attitudes, and feelings of alcoholics can literally drive us crazy if we don't put this disease in proper perspective. The drunken accusations can make us doubt ourselves and, in time, destroy our own self-confidence and self-esteem. If we have had to take on the alcoholic's responsibilities in our families in addition to our own, then we become tired and burned out from the heavy burden upon us. Many of us who lived with active alcoholism grew resentful; we longed for nurturance, love, and consideration where none was forthcoming. And if this were not enough to cope with, there were the never-ending problems that followed in the wake of active alcoholism. Partners of alcoholics are no strangers to traffic or criminal court proceedings, financial woes, police officers at the front door in the middle of the night, terrifying drives home on dark, narrow highways, embarrassment at dinner parties, hospital emergency rooms, conferences in the elementary school principal's office, and hostile stares from neighbors.

Life with an active alcoholic is very much like living too near some natural disaster, like a volcano that is always erupting and sending the surrounds into terror and chaos. Or it can be like a maelstrom that threatens to suck you and everything else that gets too near it down to certain disaster. These awful days around active alcoholism take their toll. Stress of unbelievable proportions, fear, anxiety, sorrow, rage, and unrelenting pain will eventually bring down the strongest and the best.

But while there are many reasons spouses, parents, and children of alcoholics may begin to show serious problems of their own, family members must try to keep an important thought firmly in mind: *not all the problems in the family are the result of alcoholism*. Faced with the destructive power of active alcoholism, this is a difficult if not impossible idea to accept. *Given all that has happened, we may not want to accept the possibility that we may have problems independent of our partner's alcoholism. Moreover, we may find it a great deal easier to continue to point a finger of blame at the alcoholic in our midst rather than to take a long, hard, and honest look at ourselves.*

For spouses of alcoholics, not much good will come from endless blaming of the alcoholic for our feelings and shortcomings. Even though we may have valid reasons to feel as we do, we must try to remember that when we permit the other person to control our moods, actions, and feelings of well-being, we have given them absolute power over us. In the final analysis, our moods, actions, and feelings of well-being are our own responsibilities and not those of our intoxicated spouses. We must stop giving power to the other person to manipulate our thoughts, feelings, and actions.

If we are children of alcoholics, there are things we must be willing to do. First, because of the clear genetic link, we will have to watch our own drinking very closely. At the first sign of trouble, we should be prepared to take the decisive action necessary to prevent the disease from developing in ourselves. For most children of alcoholics, this means not drinking alcohol at all, or drinking it so infrequently as not to tempt fate. Equally important is to stay aware of the constant temptation to trace all of our difficulties back to our parent's alcoholism. While we may have been influenced by this disease, we need not be victims of it unless we choose to let that happen to us. Life makes demands on all of us whether we are children of alcoholics or not. And we who were raised in alcoholic homes will have to come to grips with these challenges squarely, without resorting to excuses of any kind.

In a very real sense, the recovery from alcoholism for all members of the family is a lesson in responsibility. The alcoholic must stop blaming everybody and everything for his disease and take responsibility for his recovery. Spouses must stop blaming alcoholics for all of the problems that beset them and their families and must regain responsibility for their own lives. Children of alcoholics need to turn away from the always tempting excuse of having been reared in an alcoholic family system and to turn to renewed commitment to responsibility for their own lives.

In looking at alcoholism as a family disease, it is tempting to conclude that alcoholism is a disease of blaming. If all members of the family are to get well, each must come to understand the true nature of the disease of alcoholism and its impact on alcoholics, marriages, and families. Having gained that understanding, each member of the alcoholic family needs to take this knowledge and use it as a base upon which responsibility for his or her own life can be anchored.

CHAPTER 7

Sobriety: The Renewal of Self

As we have seen, the fourfold illness of alcoholism can destroy our bodies, minds, social worlds, and spirits. Unchecked alcoholism usually progresses to death – from an alcohol-related disease, traumatic injury, suicide, or violent incident. Fortunately, alcoholics can avoid these tragic endings. We can and do recover.

But what can we expect from recovery? Will the scars of our drinking remain with us for the rest of our lives? Can our bodies recover from the impact of heavy drinking? Will our minds ever be the same? For the vast majority of alcoholics, sobriety will return us to states of physical, mental, emotional, and spiritual health. Time is the key ingredient, however. Since we did not get into these states of illness overnight, we cannot expect to get out of them overnight. Recovery will come, but it will take time. And it will also take attention to ourselves and to those activities that will promote renewal of our physical, psychological, social, and spiritual beings.

As we now know, alcohol can impair the human body in many ways. The liver is perhaps the organ most commonly thought of when we mention alcohol-related disease. And indeed for some alcoholics who are susceptible to liver disease, there are three recognizable stages of progression.

In the first stage of alcoholic liver disease, fatty infiltration of the liver occurs. While it was previously thought that the fatty liver associated with alcoholism was caused entirely by poor eating habits and malnutrition, Dr. Charles Lieber and his colleagues at the Bronx VA Hospital showed that alcohol played a significant role. Dr. Lieber fed both rats and nonalcoholic human volunteers diets either low or high in fats along with controlled amounts of alcohol. These experiments convincingly showed that while either diet or alcohol alone could produce fat build-up in the liver, the two factors working together produced the highest fat levels.

While some authorities do not attach much significance to fatty liver, others see this condition as a step on the road to eventual serious liver disease. In any case, *if the drinker stops his intake of alcohol at this stage, he can quickly reduce the level of fat in his liver.* In effect, at this stage, sobriety can return the drinker's liver to a level of fat that is equal to his normal, alcohol-free dietary level. And this can happen very quickly. A few weeks to a few months of proper nutrition and abstinence can produce these positive changes.

If, however, the alcoholic keeps drinking, an inflammatory condition of the liver called *alcoholic hepatitis* may develop. In this stage, extensive changes in liver cells take place. Even with adequate diets, nonalcoholic volunteers given sufficient alcohol begin to show abnormalities of liver cells. Drs. Carroll Leevy, Abdul Tanribilir, and Francis Smith, specialists in the biochemistry of liver disease, point out that approximately 20 percent of alcoholic patients with very severe alcoholic hepatitis will have a progressive downhill course despite a nutritious diet and abstaining from alcohol. (Not all experts would agree with the figure of 20 percent. Some would argue that a range of one to eight percent would be more representative.) In these cases, the liver simply will not regenerate itself. Approximately one-fourth of the patients with severe alcoholic hepatitis and livers that won't regenerate have been found to respond dramatically to corrections of deficiencies in folic acid, Vitamin B_{12}, and Vitamin B_6. These vitamins are known to be necessary for DNA synthesis in the liver. In effect, the great majority of alcoholics with *alcoholic hepatitis* will recover liver function if they abstain from alcohol and receive appropriate nutritional treatments.

Cirrhosis of the liver is the final and the most grave of the alcohol-related conditions.

In cirrhosis, repeated occurrences of death of liver cells result in progressive replacement with scar tissue and only partial regeneration of cells. In time, as the alcoholism progresses, connective tissue rather than healthy liver cells makes up much of the liver tissue. When this happens, blood flow in the liver is seriously obstructed and pressure builds up. Certain veins called *esophageal varices* in the lower esophagus and extending upward or downward into the stomach may rupture. Blood loss may be extreme and sudden and, if not checked rapidly, may result in death from bleeding.

But even in this most serious condition, abstinence from alcohol can work miracles. Depending on the stage of the cirrhosis and on proper medical and nutritional management, sufficient liver function can be restored to permit many recovering alcoholics to lead normal lives. Recovery from cirrhosis is a long process, however. *No alcohol at all in any form should be taken, and expert medical advice and treatment should always be sought.*

Alcoholics do not necessarily pass through these three stages before developing cirrhosis. Certain Japanese and European alcoholics appear to develop cirrhosis without going through alcoholic hepatitis first. Moreover, only 30 percent of male alcoholics with alcoholic hepatitis go on to cirrhosis. Roughly 50 percent of females, however, progress to cirrhosis from alcoholic hepatitis. Genetic factors may be involved.

An alcoholic drinking bout can drastically lower the level of sugar in the blood. As Dr. Ronald Arky has pointed out, this precipitous plunge of the level of glucose in the blood after consumption of large amounts of alcohol can occur in persons of all ages. Young children admitted to hospital emergency rooms with accidental alcohol poisoning are routinely given intravenous glucose because the blood sugar can fall to dangerously low levels. Hypoglycemic coma, seizure, and abnormal neurological symptoms can appear. In otherwise healthy adolescents, sufficient intake of alcohol can result in a sharp lowering of the blood sugar with symptoms that can actually mimic intoxication—unsteadiness, dizziness, slurred speech, irritability, and personality changes. For some alcoholics, these problems with unstable blood sugar levels can persist well into recovery. How many alcoholics have continuing hypoglycemic problems in recovery is not known with scientific certainty (see Chapter 10). However, because of the kinds of symptoms that are associated with low blood sugar, recovering people should snack on nutritious foods throughout the day. In fact, in order to maintain an even blood sugar level, they should try to eat six or seven smaller meals a day and to avoid gorging themselves on large meals with long periods of fasting in between. Also, since "rebound" dips in the blood sugar level can occur after consuming stimulants like coffee, tea, and nicotine, as well as after eating refined sugar products, recovering people should try to minimize consumption of these substances.

In diabetic people, alcohol can have the opposite effect, and instead of resulting in a drop in blood sugar it will lead to a further rise. If the drinking has led to *acute pancreatitis* (severe inflamation of the pancreas), *diabetes* and hyperglycemia will appear. According to Dr. Ronald Arky, this form of diabetes is usually transient and will persist in only five percent of the cases.

Recovery from this form of diabetes is quite common.

Diabetic alcoholics of all types, however, must recognize that they will not be able to control their disease at all if their drinking continues. Not only are they unable to maintain their diets, their resistance to insulin goes up and control of the diabetes through medication becomes very difficult. If, however, the drinking stops and good dietary habits are maintained, many alcoholic diabetics may find that they will be able to control their diabetes through diet alone, or at least be able to reduce their need for medication. Since dietary control of diabetes has been shown to result in fewer long-term complications of the disease than occur with medication, the dietary control possible in sobriety is especially valuable.

Hypertension, or high blood pressure, is another illness that usually responds favorably to recovery from alcoholism. Depending on the source of the problem, often the blood pressure can be maintained at quite acceptable levels through complete and total sobriety and changes in lifestyle alone. Many recovering alcoholics have found that medications that reduce blood pressure may either be stopped completely or reduced significantly once they stop drinking alcohol. That this should come as a surprise to many people—including physicians who treat these problems—is difficult to understand, since it is now well-established that heavy drinking is strongly related to high blood pressure. In fact, heavy drinking is one of the more important but least recognized factors in high blood pressure.

Depending on whether or not complicating factors such as malnutrition, vomiting, and diarrhea are involved, alcoholics can show moderate to severe losses of sodium, potassium, and chloride. Magnesium may fall to very low levels as well. As Drs. James Beard and David Knott have pointed out, when these complicating factors are not present, alcoholics tend to be *overhydrated*, not dehydrated. Moreover, sodium, potassium, and chloride may be retained rather than lost from the body. In this latter case, these important *electrolytes* get distributed abnormally in the fluid spaces within the cells of the body and between the cells. As a result, there may be various disturbances in *cardiac rhythm* as well as other cardiovascular problems. In fact, heartbeat irregularities are common in intoxicated individuals, and some cases of sudden cardiac death in young adults have been thought to involve the direct effect of alcohol on heart muscle. In persons with existing heart disease, even small amounts of alcohol (two beers or two shots or two glasses of wine) can lower the ability of the heart to pump the blood. Heavy drinking can even cause complete heart block and death. In the absence of heart disease, *sobriety can rather quickly reduce these cardiac risk factors*. Sobriety obviously cannot make advanced heart or coronary artery disease go away, but it can improve a person's chances for survival.

In *cardiomyopathy* (a disease of the heart muscle, the myocardium), the heart loses its contractile force, its ability to pump the blood vigorously throughout the body. Developing slowly and insidiously in heavy drinkers over at least ten years of drinking, the symptoms of cardiomyopathy are shortness of breath, chest pain, fatigue, blood-stained sputum, and fluid retention. *In cardiomyopathy that is alcohol-related, prospects of recovery are reasonably good but will take at least five years. Of course, the alcoholic must stay completely sober for the benefits to be realized.*

There is some evidence that extremely moderate drinking may be associated statistically with the lowest rates of coronary artery disease. Alcoholics should interpret this finding with caution, because they cannot drink moderately. This finding does not, however, apply to persons with pre-existing cardiac disease.

In short, sobriety will contribute to cardiac health in alcoholics who have essentially healthy hearts, as well as those who have heart disease. For certain cardiac risk factors, improvement begins early upon abstinence from alcohol. As soon as the person is detoxified, cardiac risks associated with electrolyte imbalances, intoxication, magnesium deficiencies, and the acute effects of alcohol on the heart are reduced dramatically. For other cardiac risk factors, longer-term sobriety combined with sensible exercise and proper diets is clearly of benefit in the vast majority of cases.

Many recovering alcoholic people worry about their intellectual abilities and whether or not they have done irreversible damage to their brains by drinking. An alcoholic life can cause damage to the brain in two ways. First, there is the direct assault of alcohol on brain cells. *Alcohol is neurotoxic. This means it can cause both actual brain damage and various kinds of learning and memory deficits.* Various studies have now convincingly shown certain pathological brain changes in alcoholic patients in relatively early stages of the disease. On brain scans, there is clear evidence of enlarged *ventricles* and widened *sulci*. The ventricles are the cavities in the brain which are filled with cerebrospinal fluid. The sulci are the valleys in the external convolutions of the cerebral cortex. Enlarged ventricles and widened sulci are signs of brain atrophy (loss of brain cells).

The second source of impairment is *nutritional*. Alcoholics may fail to eat properly and, as a result, end up with severe thiamine (Vitamin B_1) deficiencies. Moreover, alcohol can directly interfere with the absorption of thiamine from the gastrointestinal system. Longstanding thiamine deficiency in addition to the direct effects of years of heavy alcohol consumption on the brain can result in either *Wernicke's encephalopathy* or *Korsakoff's psychosis*. Both are extremely grave brain disorders. *Most alcoholics do not develop these tragic advanced brain diseases.* While improvement in certain symptoms can be seen in two or three weeks with Vitamin B₁ treatment, the person with Wernicke's encephalopathy will continue to show severe memory impairment. The Korsakoff's psychosis patient rarely improves.

The memory disorders in both of these alcohol-related diseases are of two types: difficulty in remembering recent (but not long ago) events, and extreme difficulty in learning new information.

Fortunately, with complete and continuous sobriety, most recovering alcoholics will avoid these serious brain diseases entirely and will show considerable improvement in neuropsychological functioning over time. In six scientific studies that followed alcoholics over periods of one to six months of recovery, significant improvement was found in intellectual abilities in four of the six studies. In six other studies that followed alcoholics over a one year period, four gave evidence of significant improvement. Especially significant were improvements in abstracting ability and visual-perceptual motor abilities.

Scientific study has suggested that age is a critical factor in how much brain damage and intellectual dysfunction occurs in alcoholics. While both younger and older alcoholics show more deficits on neuropsychological tests of intellectual abilities compared to nonalcoholics, older alcoholics seem particularly vulnerable to the effects of alcohol. Psychologist Dr. Nelson Butters and others have suggested that with increasing age, there may be changes in our ability to metabolize alcohol. Moreover, alcohol may interfere with certain regenerative processes in the central nervous system.

A recent study using actual brain scans on alcoholics by Dr. M. A. Ron and his associates indicates that alcoholics do differ significantly from nonalcoholics on brain measurements. *However, in follow-up tests ranging from five weeks to three years, abstinent patients showed significant improvements in brain scan measurements. Drinking alcoholics, however, continued to show no improvement with regard to abnormal brain scans.* The longer the patients were abstinent, the more their condition improved.

In general, then, as far as the body is concerned, sobriety enables most alcoholics to recover important functions. Even where extreme damage has occurred, abstention from alcohol, changes in lifestyle, good eating habits, and moderate exercise has helped many. Obviously, a person who is troubled by recurrent attacks of kidney infections, for instance, must remain sober, since tissue loss in the kidneys during these attacks is greater in drinking alcoholics than in sober persons. In fact, in drinking alcoholics the tissue loss in the kidneys is about twenty times the rate in nonalcoholics or sober persons.

Because alcohol can cause atrophy of the testicles in men, lowered levels of male hormones and increased production of female hormones begin to take place in the alcoholic male. This can be seen clearly in alcoholic men with liver disease, 50 percent of whom develop female pubic hair patterns, while mammary glands are enlarged in 20 percent.

Alcohol causes a transient impotence for many men. Male sexual dysfunction can occur with heavy drinking in otherwise healthy men, and studies have shown that seven drinks can significantly reduce plasma levels of male sexual hormones.

Female alcoholics do not develop male characteristics, but they do show many hormonal changes that interfere with menstruation, fertility, and feminine fat distribution patterns in the breast and pelvic areas. Hormone levels of progesterone and estradiol – sex hormones involved in ovulation – drop in the female alcoholic.

Both males and females show defects in brain control of many hormone levels, in addition to the sex hormones. The pituitary gland is controlled by a brain center called the hypothalamus. The adrenal gland is in turn controlled by the pituitary. This interconnected network, the *Hypothalamic-Pituitary-Adrenal Axis*, is directly involved in the body's response to stress and in the production of important body steroids. Alcohol can interfere with this very important axis and affect many systems and functions.

The thyroid gland is negatively affected by alcohol. Growth hormone release is blocked. The body's antidiuretic hormone is inhibited, causing frequent urination. Calcium levels fall, which suggests that alcohol may interfere with the parathyroid hormone that controls blood calcium level.

Most of these hormonal dysfunctions caused by excessive drinking will respond very favorably to sobriety, however. Sexual activity may seem awkward and strange when the alcoholic is first sober, but barring serious physical damage to various systems, sobriety should improve sexual life for most people. *When sexual dysfunctions persist in sobriety, alcoholic people should consult therapists who specialize in both the physical and psychological aspects of sexuality.*

While sobriety can do amazing things for our bodies, it can also alter our psychological beings in major ways. People change in sobriety. Patterns of behavior frequently show 180° turns. Values change as do emotional reactions. Once people stop soaking their brains in a depressant chemical, they usually stop doing troublesome and crazy things. *Not all alcoholics have done these things, but here are some of the actions that recovering alcoholics as a group no longer do when sober:* drive drunk, fight in bars, commit domestic violence, appear in court, go to jail, end up in emergency rooms, argue with neighbors, make complete fools of themselves at parties, rob people, report for work drunk, attempt suicide, shoplift, panhandle, fight with subordinates or bosses, neglect their kids, shoot people, miss work, crash cars, accidentally start fires, drive their spouses crazy, threaten strangers, smash furniture, break windows, keep the neighbors up, go to work with hangovers, go in and out of hospitals, consume large amounts of drugs and medications, burn holes in the carpets and furniture, fall overboard, get beaten up, fight with police, pass out on the floor, crash planes, boats, and trucks, sleep past their stops on trains, wreck machines, miss airplanes, fall into the soup, misplace their automobiles, forget appointments, go to prison, and never cut the grass.

Obviously, sobriety changes many patterns of behavior for the better.

Sobriety can lead to resolutions of marital and family problems that have plagued us for years. This does not mean that all sober alcoholic families and marriages will be happy—or even that they will survive. In some cases, sobriety gives couples the freedom to pull apart as well as to move closer together. People who came together in the years when alcoholism was active may find they have little reason to stay together in sobriety. Sadly, some couples will find that the drinking years were simply too destructive to the relationship; the hurt and pain may be too deep to go away. While such marriages may be beyond repair, sobriety will at least permit them to end in dignity, with a minimum of rancor, bitterness, and further destruction of self-esteem.

For the most part, however, sobriety can usher in periods of mutual respect, growth, and understanding in many alcoholic marriages and families. This can be especially true of couples who seek outside professional help when it is necessary and who also maintain active involvement in AA, Al-Anon, and in Alateen for the children.

Attitudes, beliefs, ideas, and thinking processes are the first things to show positive changes in recovery. In only a few months to a year of abstention from alcohol and other drugs, alcoholics will usually show appropriate attitudes toward others—their families, employers, and communities. The thinking also clears up fairly rapidly. Once the alcohol and other drugs are out of the system, most alcoholics begin to think more realistically almost right away. Thought processes become more orderly and rational, and the somewhat "crazy" ideas of the active alcoholic stage are replaced with reasonable beliefs and convictions. Intellectual abilities will return to normal within a year for most alcoholics in earlier stages of the disease. Certain abilities in some late-stage alcoholics may take much longer. (If damage is extensive, some abilities may never return. Fortunately, relatively few alcoholics will be so affected.)

Alcoholics whose livelihoods depended on creative processes may find the return to productive work particularly difficult in early sobriety. Poetry that flowed from the poet's pen with some lubrication from wine, beer, or Irish whiskey won't come so easily sober. Creative jazz musicians may find it odd to strike up the band in some smoky nightclub where everybody is drinking but them. Musical ideas that poured out of horns when the players were mellow on drinks and marijuana seem to dry up with sobriety. Visual artists may have relied heavily on hallucinogens of various kinds (marijuana, mescaline, LSD, hashish) for their unique perceptions. Actors may have grown accustomed to a couple of stiff ones before going onstage or before the motion picture cameras.

There really isn't much question about it: alcohol and the creative arts do seem to go together. American literature, for example, reads like a "who's who" of alcoholism. Of eight Americans who were awarded the Nobel Prize for Literature, five were clearly alcoholic—or such problematic and heavy drinkers that they would be diagnosed alcoholic by current standards. The drinking of Eugene O'Neill was legendary. William Faulkner and John Steinbeck had their problems, as did Sinclair Lewis and Ernest Hemingway. Numerous other major American writers were literally destroyed or their lives complicated greatly by their alcoholism or problematic drinking: Scott Fitzgerald, Edgar Allen Poe, Malcolm Lowry, Hart Crane, John Berryman, Thomas Wolfe, Tennessee Williams, Truman Capote, Ambrose Bierce, John Cheever, John O'Hara, and Edmund Wilson.

The list of the artistically talented and alcoholic is long indeed!

What can such imaginative and inventive alcoholics expect from recovery? Will they lose their creativity forever? Must they be high, stoned, or drugged to write fiction, edit films, play jazz, construct novels, make up short stories, sing the blues, and paint?

The answer is that nobody knows for sure, but the creativity of most individuals will not dry up, but it may take different form with sobriety from alcohol and other drugs. One thing that is fairly certain, however, is that creative processes will not immediately blossom in sobriety. Recovering alcoholic artists should prepare themselves for a period of adjustment that could be quite lengthy in some cases. As modern research shows, we tend to perform a task best in the state we were in when we first learned it. This phenomenon is called *state dependent learning*. It suggests that if we learned and practiced a skill like jazz trumpet playing while under the influence of alcohol and other drugs, we are likely to play our most inventive and imaginative "riffs" while under the same degree of influence.

Because of state dependent learning, it will take time for creative activities to re-emerge in sobriety. Creative recovering alcoholics should not be discouraged by the seeming barrenness of early sobriety. In time, creativity will return, and it will be strong, enduring, and particularly brilliant in sobriety. *Above all else, creative alcoholics struggling with their crafts in early recovery should not overlook one fact: their creativity is in them and not in a bottle, a joint, or a line of cocaine.*

While intellectual things seem to come back rather quickly in sobriety, emotions and feelings take a lot longer. Some alcoholics bounce around a great deal before their feelings stabilize. Moods swing from high to low with alarming regularity for these people. (If such swings in elation and depression do not end in the first few months of recovery, professional help should be sought. Such variations in mood may indicate an underlying *affective disorder* which had been masked by the drinking.)

In early sobriety recovering alcoholics may find that they cannot get their emotions under control. They react to people, events, and situations with an intensity that is just too extreme. There is too much anger. Too much fear. Too much sorrow. There can even be too much joy and euphoria in early recovery!

Many alcoholics will find that it will take several years to begin to get these troublesome emotional reactions under control. We alcoholics are very sensitive people. Our feelings are hurt easily because of our low self-esteem. We can feel rejected because of the smallest things. And we can take on guilt and responsibility for the sad state of the universe if somebody asks us to. Or we can stifle our emotions so much that in early recovery we have no emotions at all and feel dead and empty inside.

Unfortunately, there simply is no quick and easy way to emotional health and well-being for all people—nonalcoholics as well as alcoholic. Reactions learned early in life are difficult to change whether we have a drinking problem or not. But there are things that can help us in our recovery.

First, alcoholics need to get one thing firmly in mind. *Our emotional reactions are not the cause of our alcoholism. In fact, they are most likely a further complication or outcome of our alcoholism.* Just as liver disease is a complication of alcoholism, a negative self-concept is also a complication or outcome of the disease. As a result of the repeated assaults on our self-images by our drunken thoughts, beliefs, and actions, we have come to think poorly of ourselves. Because our emotional reactions can lead us to pick up the first drink, however, we do have to get them under control. Remember that a reaction to a situation or person can't make us drink. Only we can make ourselves drink. *Feelings are facts of life, but they need not be a fact of drinking unless we choose to make them so.*

Second, most of us will need help with our emotional reactions. Fortunately, help is available in a variety of forms. Psychotherapy with knowledgeable psychologists, psychiatrists, or social workers can give us perspective on some of our problems with feelings. For those who do not care for psychotherapeutic professional assistance, other approaches can be tried. Physical exercise is of great benefit regardless of what one chooses to do. Regular jogging, aerobic dancing, walking, tennis, workouts with fitness equipment, competitive sports, and so forth can do wonders for stress, tension, frustration, anger, and depression.

Massage, whirlpool, swimming, and steam baths are also excellent ways to get rid of the tension that frequently underlies an inappropriate reaction to a particular situation or person. If we find ourselves "burning out" on our jobs, treating ourselves to the luxury of a steam bath and a full-body massage is one way to find some immediate relief while we are searching for long-term solutions. We need to be kind to ourselves, with frequent recreations and vacations in sobriety rather than overwork and long hours. Too many of us recovering people become workaholics, and compulsive work activities take the place of drinking!

Meditation, spiritual retreats, and religious activities can also help some people in the early stages of recovery. These spiritually-centered activities give us the larger vision we so desperately need to get out of ourselves and to put the myriad petty but draining details of our worlds in proper perspective.

Serious involvement in Alcoholics Anonymous is perhaps the single most important thing we can do for our emotional lives. There is a healing power in community that simply does not come when we try to go it alone. As many people outside of Alcoholics Anonymous do not know, AA is not only a program of recovery; it is a *fellowship* of women and men who "share their experience, strength, and hope with each other." What one alcoholic cannot do alone, many can accomplish. This fact has been proven time and time again in Alcoholics Anonymous, a program and fellowship in which the miraculous is made commonplace.

There are various attitudes and techniques that a person can use to lessen some of these troublesome emotional reactions that persist into sobriety. As many members of AA can testify, *time binding* concepts can really help. Life is just too large an item to deal with except on a daily, twenty-four-hour basis. Time boggles the mind as much as Einstein's theory of relativity. How can we locate ourselves in such a vast sea of time and life happenings? Perhaps the only way to do it is to take life twenty-four hours at a time. What seems impossible as an issue of a lifetime yields rapidly on a day-at-a-time basis.

When we stop and consider time, it is amazing how much of our emotional lives are caught up with our psychological pasts and our psychological futures. Many of us are consumed by guilt over worlds that no longer exist—and may never have existed. Like historians of ourselves we construct our biographies from bits and pieces of actual happenings. The real past is certainly there. But so is the *imagined past*—the biographies we construct from the mosaic of dimly remembered happenings.

Just as each of us has an imagined past, we also have an *imagined future*. There most certainly is a future that waits patiently in time for each of us, but all that we know of it is what we imagine. When our futures arrive, they rarely are as we imagined them. Despite this fact, we continue to worry and fret over events that *may* happen, over things that are weeks, months, and even years ahead. In effect, we make ourselves sick with anxiety and future dread.

What we fail to realize in all of this "time travel" is that without our psychological pasts we cannot be consumed by guilt, and without our psychological futures, we cannot be paralyzed by anxiety.

We alcoholics need not be victims of our biographies, nor do we need to be tyrannized by our anxious visions of things to come. We can live in the here-and-now of the reality of each day as it unfolds. Not only can we live in reality, we will be more than capable of dealing with it, with a degree of serenity and peace that may surprise us.

It is useful also to learn to give oneself various commands. These self-commands can take many forms. *Relax and take it easy* is a useful self-command when we find ourselves getting tense. *Slow down* is another one. In AA, people remind themselves to get quiet with *Easy does it*. For obsessions, *Stop thinking about this!* is sometimes helpful, as is *This is no big deal* for anxiety-provoking events.

Anagrams in which letters remind us of key words in particular self-commands are helpful to some persons. HALT is one such anagram, which reminds the person not to get too *hungry, angry, lonely,* or *tired*. RELAX is one I've found useful. It stands for *recreate, energize, love, accept,* and *examine*. In recovery we need to find ways to renew ourselves, mobilize our energies toward reasonable goals, find time to love ourselves and others, accept the things about ourselves and our worlds that we cannot change, and examine our ways carefully for the truth about ourselves.

Just as it is helpful to stop and locate ourselves in time, realizing our position in *space* is good too. On busy days, we rush from one situation to another without realizing it. As our locations change, so do the actors, pace, mood, and plot. Forgetting that we are no longer in the office, we may run home and treat our families like our employees or coworkers. Or we may rush from an important business meeting to a quiet supper with friends, but not take the necessary steps to "decompress." Sometimes we come from encounters with angry, hostile people and forget to take time to shake off all that anger before we walk in our front doors.

In many of these transactions that we go in and out of, it is extremely useful to take a quiet moment, stop the busy flow of our minds and activities, and remind ourselves that we have left situation A and are about to enter situation B. Mentally focussing on the new situation in a relaxed state can ease the transition and reduce stress and tension considerably.

Still another way to control our emotional reactions is to use *creative imagery*. In this technique we focus on a feared situation or one that might make us angry, and then we practice the opposite. If we are afraid of failing in a situation, we imagine ourselves in the situation and succeeding. If we think we will become inappropriately angry in a situation, we might try mental rehearsals in which we picture ourselves as calm, cheerful, and serene.

Creative imagery is a very useful exercise for any situation that we find emotionally troubling. Instead of mentally rehearsing *failure* as we typically do, why not try mental rehearsals of *success*? We sometimes bring about the worlds we imagine by our very imaginings, so why not try a positive image of the world and ourselves rather than a negative one?

Just as our emotional renewal in sobriety may take years, certain of our social relationships may require much patience and a great deal of work. *As a rule, relationships that are more distant and less intimate will improve first.* In early sobriety we will probably get along with strangers almost immediately, but our relationships with our children and spouses will take much longer to improve. If we go to Alcoholics Anonymous, we will likely establish warm, trusting relationships with new friends within a few weeks or months. But our relationships to our lovers or parents may continue to be very strained and marred by distrust, anger, and fear.

We alcoholics must remember that the persons who were hurt most by our alcoholism were usually ourselves and the people with whom we were the most intimate. Many times we apologized for the pain and suffering we caused our loved ones, and we promised that we wouldn't drink again. Our disease, however, would not let us keep our promises, and we left a trail of broken promises, distrust, and fear in our wakes. It is small wonder that when we finally do succeed in getting sober, our loved ones are likely to take a cautious position and a wait-and-see attitude. We must remember that their fear is realistic, and not unfair or insulting to us. Just as we will need time for our recoveries to progress, our loved ones will need time to deal with their reactions to our past drinking careers. They will also require much more than our *words* for reassurance. It is our *sober actions* that will assure our loved ones that this time we truly mean what we say. We will have to walk like we talk if we expect the people we love to have confidence in our newly found sobriety. Until they are able once again to place their trust in us, we must be patient and accepting rather than angry and resentful.

In general, then, the renewal of our social selves will follow this general course: relationships with distant people will improve first; and then more slowly, we will find ourselves able to repair and renew our most intimate and important relationships. In some cases, however, we alcoholics must be prepared to accept the fact that our disease will have gone too far. No matter how good our intentions, how sincere our amends, and how earnestly we wish to continue to be in intimate relation to a particular loved one, the destructive power of our disease will have damaged that relationship beyond repair. There may be such "scar tissue" in the relationship that no amount of well-meaning action and sincere effort on our parts can heal it; the relationship will never be mended. In this instance we will have been given our first true opportunity in sobriety to act in a genuinely mature manner and to accept what is inevitable with some degree of serenity, grace, and respect for both ourselves and the other.

Finally, in addition to renewal of our physical, psychological, and social beings, sobriety allows us to renew our spiritual beings. One might say that "discover" would be a better word than "renew," but alcoholics do not have to dream up or invent a spiritual life. For each of us, there is a god within. There has always been a god within. In sobriety, it is our task to renew our relationship with this god within each of us.

As our sobriety deepens, we turn to the god within each of us for comfort, guidance, and meaning. For the Greeks, it meant turning to *en theos*, the god within. Our English word *enthusiasm* was derived from this Greek word for the inner god. Hence, in sobriety, we turn to enthusiasm rather than to despair, cynicism, or anger. And enthusiasm is simply another word for love. When we are enthusiastic about life, we love life. And when we say we are enthusiastic about a book, a song, or a beautiful morning, it is just another way of saying we love these things.

In sobriety, then, we turn inevitably to the god within, to enthusiasm, to love. Like flowers turning to the sun, children turning to the sounds of laughter, and the darkest night turning to day, we turn to love. And in turning to the love inside ourselves, we come to know the love inside others. Then it is only a matter of all of us turning together in time.

Of all the miraculous renewals of self through sobriety, none shines so brightly or with such glory as the renewal of love.

CHAPTER 8

Not Only in Bottles

Alcohol isn't the only drug that poses problems for alcoholics. Since the decade of the 1960s, when mood-altering chemicals of all kinds swept through many modern societies, alcoholics in ever-increasing numbers have shown difficulties with one or more drugs in addition to alcohol. Marijuana, cocaine, quaaludes, amphetamines, tranquilizers, codeine—these are but a few of the drugs that are now affecting more and more alcoholics. Younger alcoholics in particular seem attracted to these other substances.

From the outset, however, it is important to point out that many alcoholics do not show a history of dependence on any drug except alcohol. Many old-timers in AA drank alcoholically but never got involved with anything else. Moreover, in a society in which experimentation with drugs is widespread and even perhaps expected as a part of social development, it is not surprising to find many current alcoholics trying various substances. Experimentation, however, is not dependence or "abuse" in the various meanings of that poorly defined and indiscriminately applied term.

Alcoholics should not, unless required for medical reasons, use psychoactive substances. But just because an alcoholic has tried a given substance—or even used it on and off—does not mean he or she is dependent on the substance. Nearly 70 percent of the American people drink alcohol, yet only one out of ten of these drinkers shows problems or becomes dependent upon the drug. Not everybody who drinks is an alcoholic. Not everybody who has ever smoked a joint of marijuana is a drug addict.

There are, of course, plenty of persons around who are *polydrug* dependent—they are dependent on one or more drugs, including alcohol. But there are also a great many "pure alcoholics." These are people who may have experimented or not with various chemicals at times in their developmental histories, but have never really used anything but alcohol.

While we personally may not have been involved with other drugs, it is important that we understand these other chemicals for several reasons. First, the fact that we have never been dependent on other drugs doesn't mean we couldn't become dependent at some point in the future. Some people have made progress in their recoveries from alcoholism but have foolishly turned to other chemicals like tranquilizers to help them relax. These people are playing with the fire of a second addiction, often without realizing it. Knowledge about drugs may help all of us to prevent such unhappy outcomes.

Second, while we may not personally have been involved with drugs and would not dream of doing so in the future, we may find ourselves in an important relationship with someone who is using drugs destructively. Our children, for example, may start out using drugs, not alcohol. They might mix alcohol with drugs—a particularly dangerous practice. People with whom we are working and trying to help in programs like AA may have a problem involving several chemicals in addition to alcohol. And some of us may find, when we sober up, that our spouses or lovers have serious drug problems of their own, which have gone unnoticed while the relationship has been clouded by our problematic drinking.

Finally, alcoholics should make it a practice to find out all that they can about both prescription and non-prescription drugs. In the sober alcoholic, chemicals of various kinds may have the undesirable outcome of triggering off craving for alcohol. In the drinking alcoholic, certain chemicals may mix dangerously with alcohol.

In thinking about drugs generally, *tolerance* is an important concept to know about. Tolerance refers to how much of a drug your body can tolerate without showing physical or behavioral problems. When you find yourself needing more and more of the chemical in order to get the same effect, then your tolerance has increased. Tolerance is to some extent a genetically determined thing in that some people show either very little or very great tolerance to alcohol practically from the start of their drinking lives. Alcoholics may be people who are naturally resistant to the effects of alcohol early in their drinking careers. It was often the alcoholic who drank in the beginning like he had a "hollow leg" or could "drink everybody under the table." In time, of course, this high level of tolerance gives way to reduced tolerance as alcoholics get older and as their disease progresses.

Cross-tolerance refers to the interesting fact that while you are building tolerance to one drug you are taking you may also be increasing your tolerance to some other drug you are not taking. Generally, cross-tolerance occurs *only* to drugs that are in the same pharmacological class. You can, for example, show cross-tolerance to Valium if you have been drinking alcohol steadily for some weeks, because Valium and alcohol are in the same class of drugs—depressants. As a rule, you won't show tolerance to cocaine just because you have been in a period of heavy drinking. Cocaine is a stimulant while alcohol is a depressant. As drugs of different pharmacological classes, they are not cross-tolerant.

Physical dependence on alcohol or another drug has occurred when you experience withdrawal signs on trying to stop drinking or using. Withdrawal signs in alcoholism can be subtle and mild, consisting only of some inner shakiness, slightly increased pulse rate, slightly elevated blood pressure, mild depression, and some anxiety. On the other hand, withdrawal signs can be severe and dramatic; they can consist of bizarre hallucinations, seizures, obvious shaking of the hands, highly elevated blood pressure, and rapid pulse. When we alcoholics reach the stage of severe physical dependence, we have traveled very far down the road into alcoholism. An important thing to remember, however, is that withdrawal signs need not be extreme for you to be an alcoholic or to be physically dependent on alcohol.

When we drink and use drugs at the same time, we risk exposure to the dangerous effects of *drug synergy*. Due to synergy, drugs and alcohol do not combine in a simple additive way. Rather, the drugs and alcohol *multiply* each other's effects. For example, four drinks of alcohol in combination with three Valiums does not simply add up to seven. It isn't $4 + 3 = 7$, but perhaps $4 \times 3 = 12$. Drugs in the same class are particularly dangerous together. Mixing alcohol and barbiturates like phenobarbital can kill alcoholics and, in fact, has. Death from synergy often comes from complete suppression of respiratory centers in the brain.

Alcohol can mix synergistically with a number of medications. Loss of consciousness and serious, life-threatening conditions can result from combining alcohol with the antihistamines we take for head colds and allergies of various kinds. The same thing can happen if we drink on top of Seconal, Percodan, codeine, Thorazine, or any of the other barbiturate, narcotic or phenothiazine drugs. Alcohol added to certain antidepressants called MAO inhibitors can raise blood pressure to a life-threatening level. Flushing, headaches, nausea, vomiting, chest pain, and abdominal gas can be produced by drinking while taking any of the following: *Flagyl*, a medication used to treat vaginal yeast infections; *Fulvicin*, an antifungal medication; oral anti-diabetics such as *Orinase*.

Mixed with *aspirin*, alcohol can cause stomach bleeding. This problem can occur with any aspirin-containing medication including Anacin, Aspergum, Bayer, Bufferin, Arthritis Pain Formula, Congestion, Coricidin, Empirin, Excedrin, Midol, Vanquish.

If you are taking blood anticoagulants such as Coumadin, Dicumarol, Liquamar, Miradon, Panwarfin, or Sintrom you should not drink alcohol because it will eliminate or reduce the effect of the medication. It is also not a good idea to drink during a course of antibiotic therapy. And since alcohol can have effects on our cardiovascular systems, drinking while taking any blood pressure or heart medication is really not a good idea. Alcohol alone usually results in a rise in blood pressure, an increased workload on the heart, and possible disturbances in the heart's rhythm. These are the symptoms we take cardiac medications for in the first place.

Alcohol can dissolve the outer coating on time-release medications like those used for cold or diet capsules. This may result in a single very large dose rather than continuous small amounts of medication released into the body over time.

Since we alcoholics tend to smoke a lot, it is probably in order to mention that smoking doesn't go with medications either. With oral contraceptives smoking increases the risk of blood clotting. The effects of many medications are reduced in smokers since smoking leads to faster elimination of certain medications from the body. Some of these medications are as follows: cardiac and blood pressure medications, insulin, anti-inflammatory nonsteroidal agents, antiasthma drugs containing theophylline, antidepressant medications, pain killers such as Darvon, and major tranquilizers for several mental illnesses.

All in all, if we must take any medications, it is a very good idea not to drink alcohol in any amount, and it is probably wise to cut back on our smoking or eliminate it entirely.

In understanding drugs, it is quite important to grasp the concept of drug *half-life*. The half-life of a drug is the amount of time it will take for one-half of the original dose to be metabolized in our bodies. If, for example, we take four 5mg tablets of Valium on Monday, come Tuesday morning we won't have zero drug in our bodies, but perhaps as much as 5mg remaining. If we take another 20mg of Valium throughout the day on Tuesday, we will have 25mg in our bodies. By Wednesday morning, perhaps 10mg of the drug is still in our systems. Adding 20mg to it again, as we might on a doctor's prescription, we accumulate still higher levels of drug in our bodies. The half-life of drugs, then, is one often overlooked factor that practically insures continued presence of the drugs in our systems longer than we might think. Because of drug half-life we typically reach higher levels of drugs in our bodies than a simple sum of total milligrams each day might suggest.

In addition to half-life of the drug itself, we must also consider long-term effects of the drug. These longer-term effects that persist may be caused by continued presence of metabolites (breakdown products of the drug in our bodies) or by actual temporary changes in the brain. *One recent experiment on animals, for example, showed that the effects of high doses of amphetamine (a central nervous system stimulant) on dopamine levels in the brain were still apparent fifty days after the animals stopped receiving the drug.*

In effect, psychoactive drugs are dangerous for many reasons, but they are particularly dangerous because their effects can persist over many days after the drug-taking has ceased.

Of course, drugs are not all alike. They have different chemical structures, affect the brain differently, and show different behavioral correlations. For this reason, pharmacologists use various classification schemes to categorize the drugs.

Alcohol belongs to a class of drugs called *nonselective general depressants*. These drugs are called nonselective because they reach many sites in the body and produce widespread effects. In a way, drugs such as these could be said to have many "side effects." Alcohol, for example, goes to virtually every cell, tissue, and organ of the body. Once there, it depresses the functioning of that body cell, tissue, or organ. This is why drugs like alcohol are called "general depressants." Alcohol doesn't pep us up. It may produce an initial mild excitation of our nervous systems but that will quickly give way to sedative or "downer" effects if we continue to drink. This characteristic of initial excitement followed by sedation is true of many depressant chemicals.

Drugs in the nonselective general depressant class are as follows: alcohol, ether, Valium, Librium, Miltown, Equanil, Doriden, quaaludes, Placidyl, phenobarbital, Seconal, Nembutal, Valmid, Noludal, and all other barbiturates, including many sleeping pills. All of these drugs in this class can produce cross-tolerance and dependence. Alcoholics should not take these drugs since a second addiction is the likely result.

A second major class of drugs is the *central nervous system stimulants*. These drugs are highly dissimilar to the depressants in chemical structure, effects on the brain, and impact on behavior. Hence, they are not cross-tolerant to alcohol or other depressants, and dependence on stimulants need not imply cross-dependence to alcohol. These drugs "jack us up," "get us going," "stimulate" us. They "speed" us up.

The amphetamines ("uppers," "speed") are in this class. So is the expensive drug, cocaine, that managed to hook Dr. Sigmund Freud, the father of psychoanalysis. Amphetamines have always been considered dangerous drugs; in the street language of the 1960s, "speed kills." Cocaine is also a dangerous drug. In the past several years, the Drug Abuse Warning Network (DAWN) has reported sharp increases in the numbers of cocaine mentions in hospital emergency room data from across the nation. Young adults in particular have turned to cocaine, and at the time of this writing, cocaine is the preferred high on college and university campuses.

While we may not think of it as such, caffeine is a genuine drug, and it too can have stimulating properties. Alcoholics should monitor their coffee intake closely and take active steps to reduce it if they are drinking more than two or three cups a day. Even this much coffee may be too much for certain alcoholics with health problems. For those of us who suffer from hypoglycemia in addition to our alcoholism, even small amounts of coffee can trigger a later fall in blood sugar level and uncomfortable symptoms of irritability, sudden fatigue, headaches, dizziness, and fear. And for those of us who are afflicted by high anxiety or panic, a stimulant like coffee can precipitate episodes of psychic distress, hyperventilation, rapid heart rate, and other feelings of discomfort.

We alcoholics must stay clear of stimulants generally. The trouble with stimulants is quite clear: *these drugs can put us into highly aroused states in which we cannot relax, get to sleep, or calm down.* As a result, we may start thinking of drinking as a way to bring ourselves down to a more comfortable level of arousal. In addition, continued use of certain stimulants at high levels may so alter chemistry in our brains that we may begin to have psychotic-like episodes that in some ways mimic severe mental illness (see Chapter 4 for a discussion of cocaine, dopamine, and schizophrenia).

Hallucinogens are still another class of drugs that can spell big trouble for alcoholics. While marijuana is regarded by many users as a harmless drug, it is very dangerous to alcoholics for the simple reason that it can lead a recovering person right back to a drink. We don't smoke marijuana to get rational or linear. We generally smoke it to get "wrecked," "stoned," "high," "out of our minds," and so forth. Obviously, marijuana is not the drug of choice for getting calculus problems done, designing a skyscraper, or piloting an aircraft. Today's marijuana is a great deal more powerful than the "pot" of the 1960s. One joint of the newer hybrid "sensemilla" contains ten times the THC (the active ingredient) of yesterday's grass. (Sensemilla is Spanish for "without seeds.")

But while most people would agree you shouldn't smoke marijuana and then try to do calculus problems, some of these same people don't see the connection to trying to stay sober. You do need all of your wits about you to do calculus, to design skyscrapers, or fly a 747. But you also need all of your wits about you to stay sober.

Marijuana distorts our thoughts, perceptions, moods, and actions, as do other hallucinogens. When we are stoned on marijuana, we really don't have all of our wits about us. If we are in a romantic situation, with candlelight, wine, and an attractive other, it is one very short step from a joint to a drink. Moreover, since marijuana causes a dry mouth and throat, people would drink cold beer or wine along with their smokes. In time, cold alcoholic beverages became associated with a marijuana high. This is clearly not a good association for a recovering alcoholic to activate.

We should call a marijuana "high" what it really is: *marijuana intoxication*. When we suck marijuana into our lungs and its active ingredient tetra-hydrocannabinol (THC) finds its way to our brains, we are *drunk*. Perhaps we are not drunk on alcohol, but we are drunk. People trying to recover from alcoholism should grasp that point and not forget it. Intoxication is intoxication, no matter what we call it or where it comes from.

Along with staying away from marijuana, alcoholics should stay very clear of the other hallucinogens. These include LSD, peyote, mescaline, psilocybin, and PCP or "angel dust." Marijuana and PCP are fat-soluble drugs. This means that they will enter neural tissue and remain there for fairly long periods. For heavy marijuana smokers, THC will be detectable in urine for as much as eighteen days after intake has been stopped.

Despite earlier interest in treating alcoholism with LSD, contemporary workers in the field know from experience that LSD doesn't help alcoholics. It complicates recovery enormously. A person who has been drinking heavily and taking numerous LSD trips is often the most difficult patient to reach in a treatment center. Moreover, the risk of flashbacks (later reliving of parts of the active LSD experience) should be enough to discourage anybody— alcoholic or not—from taking this chemical. LSD not only affects the mind, it alters the brain.

Opiate narcotics comprise a group of drugs that can lead to insidious, stubborn, persistent, and dangerous addictions. From the opium poppy, we derive three natural narcotics. These are opium, morphine, and codeine. While most people know that opium and morphine are opiate narcotics, they may think of codeine as the rather innocent stuff that can come in cough syrups. Despite its seeming ordinariness, however, codeine is a highly addictive narcotic. Alcoholics especially should scrutinize physicians' prescriptions carefully when seeking medical advice for a severe cough associated with flu or a cold. It is best to let the doctor know that you don't want cough preparations that contain either alcohol or codeine.

While opium, morphine, and codeine are pure, natural narcotics, heroin is a semi-synthetic drug—it is synthesized in the laboratory from morphine. Aside from the fact that heroin can prove highly addictive for particular individuals, it can lead people to an antisocial life in which criminal behavior is the only way such an expensive habit can be maintained.

Methadone is a completely synthetic drug developed by the Germans during the Second World War. The *adone* in methadone reveals that the drug was named after Adolph Hitler. It is also called dolophine. In the United States, efforts are made to treat addicts by maintaining them on methadone for long periods of time followed by long, tapering detoxification periods. The question of the long-term success of treating drug addicts by substituting one similar drug for another is far from settled. Controversy surrounds methadone treatment, with advocates and opponents often arguing bitterly over its use in treatment. While we cannot settle this question here, we can assert with some authority that alcoholics should not go anywhere near methadone. They should refuse it on the street corner or in a clinic. And, of course, they should steer very clear of heroin, codeine, morphine, and narcotic drugs, including Dilaudid, Percodan, Demerol, and any other synthetic narcotic drug.

It is curious to note that the last big narcotics epidemic in America happened at the turn of the century and came on the heels of a cocaine epidemic! The current cocaine craze has many drug experts worried about whether or not history will repeat itself and we will be plunged again into a heroin epidemic—not a comforting thought.

Drugs of any of these classes—depressants, stimulants, hallucinogens, and narcotics—are not reliable solutions to human problems. We cannot take a drink or a pill because we are nervous and need to relax. Nor can we rely upon stimulants and the false energies they provide. Hallucinogens will simply switch our minds into irrational channels and our brains into alien and malfunctional chemistries. And narcotics will drive even the strongest among us to social ruin and despair. Why bother with any of them?

We alcoholics have to see that there are no lasting chemical solutions to life's inevitable problems. Our sciences of the future may alter this fact but, at present, there are no substitutes for personal growth and spiritual development.

It is important to note, however, that there are serious problems of mental illness from which small numbers of alcoholics may suffer greatly. These unfortunate victims of tragic illnesses in addition to their alcoholism may very well require certain medications if they are to have a hope of functioning normally. The schizophrenic alcoholic may have to take *Thorazine* or *Haldol*, neither of which is related to the chemical structures of the typical drugs of addiction we have considered in the earlier pages. Manic-depressive alcoholics may have to take *lithium* if they are to get their behavior under control. Lithium is not a drug or narcotic. It is a mineral that can alter brain chemistry. *Severely* depressed alcoholics will not recover from their depressions without expert medical treatment and antidepressant medications. This does not mean that every time an alcoholic gets depressed, he should take antidepressants. These medications are not for the usual ups and downs of alcoholics, nor for their "blues" or depressed feelings. The vast majority of alcoholics must learn to handle these common human problems without taking antidepressants. However, for the alcoholics who suffer from very severe depressions linked not to their life happenings, but to abnormalities in the chemistry of their brains, antidepressant treatment to correct these abnormalities in brain chemistry is an absolute necessity.

But aside from these special cases, there truly are no chemical solutions to life's problems. We do have to recognize that a small number of alcoholics may need medications to rebalance the chemistries of their brains because of *other* diseases.

However, while it may be appropriate to treat particular alcoholics with certain psychoactive chemicals, *it is always inappropriate to treat alcoholism per se with long-term chemical manipulation.* Science may offer a "magic bullet" someday to cure alcoholism. However, it hasn't done so yet, and given the complexities involved, it isn't likely to do so soon.

CHAPTER 9

Alcoholism at Work

In 1980, Americans spent $245 billion on health care. But as the United States Chamber of Commerce has pointed out, nearly half of this enormous sum was paid by employers as employee health benefits. With employers paying roughly $125 billion a year for the health care of their employees, American companies have a stake in alcoholism whether they realize it or not.

Health care costs for employees, however, are only a part of the picture. Absenteeism, turnover, loss of valuable employees through alcohol-related accidents, low and inferior productivity, and poor decision-making are now widely recognized as some of the costs of alcoholism to business, industry, education, and the professions. In some industrial work settings, alcohol and drugs in the parking lot over lunch hour are as much a part of the work scene as the lunch bucket. Coming to work with hangovers or still drunk from a night of heavy drinking is commonplace. Corporate decision-making after first thoroughly soaking the brain in a nonselective general depressant drug like alcohol has happened more than a few times in particular organizations. People do drink on, before, and after the job. And much of this drinking has negative results for the employees, for coworkers, and for the corporation or business.

In 1980, California, the most populous state in the nation with a total population of 24 million people, had nearly 1.4 million alcoholics and problem drinkers. Nearly 5.6 million people were adversely affected by problem drinkers, and California officials estimated costs to the state of $4.28 billion. Minnesota's Council on Health reported its 1980 costs for chemical dependency generally to be $1.4 billion.

Georgia estimated annual costs of alcoholism in 1981 of $350 million to business and industry, $217 million in hospital health care, and $13 million in law enforcement and criminal justice. Alabama in the same year placed its alcohol costs to business and industry at $477 million, while Iowa's costs were $319 million. North Carolina's industries lost $450 million in 1981, while New York's corporations probably spent over a billion dollars on alcoholism and alcohol abuse.

A pioneering study at Oldsmobile's Lansing, Michigan, plant in 1975 showed what business and industry could do to reduce alcohol-related costs. In this study, ninety-nine hourly workers with alcohol problems and eighteen with drug problems were studied prior to treatment and after treatment. At the same time, a group of twenty-four workers with alcohol and drug problems which were not treated were also followed.

Following treatment for alcoholism, the group of alcoholics who received alcoholism treatment showed a 52 percent reduction in lost man-hours. At the same time, the group who did not get treatment showed a ten percent *increase* in lost man-hours. In terms of dollars, these lost man-hours amounted to a gain of $233,000 for the alcoholics who got treatment and a loss of $7,000 for those who did not. Sickness benefits decreased by $13,000 for the treated alcoholics while these benefits increased by over $8,000 for the untreated group.

Since this early study at Oldsmobile, many studies have shown that employers are smart to set up programs for identifying alcoholics and helping them to get treatment. It costs a great deal of money to replace experienced, skilled, and knowledgeable personnel. Why fire good workers when treatment can restore their value to their company? As the studies have shown, it is considerably less costly to rehabilitate alcoholic workers than it is to recruit and train new people. At Kennecott Copper Company, absenteeism was reduced by 52 percent by a company program that helped alcoholics get into treatment. An occupational alcoholism program at New York Telephone was estimated to save the company $1.5 million, while programs at seven railroad companies, General Motors, and the Police and Fire Departments of the City of Philadelphia all reported significant drops in the costs of alcoholism associated with absenteeism and lowered productivity. At General Motors, about 42,000 workers (seven percent of the GM North American work force) were involved in the company's Employee Assistance Program. Of these 42,000 troubled GM workers, 25,200 had alcohol problems. For these troubled workers, participation in the Employee Assistance Program reduced time off the job by 40 percent, and sickness and accident benefit payments by 60 percent.

With regard to sickness and accident benefits, Illinois Bell Telephone Company found that treating alcoholics not only made good humanitarian sense, it also made good "dollars and sense." The company reported a savings of $1,000 per treated employee in sickness and accident disability payments. Kennecott Copper found that hospital, medical, and surgical costs dropped by 48 percent in the group of alcoholics that received treatment.

Today, more and more companies have recognized that it is smart to rehabilitate alcoholics rather than replace them. Employee Assistance Programs that help workers with a variety of problems including alcoholism are now a familiar part of the industrial and business scene. These programs are designed to see that alcoholics get treatment and are returned to the work force as productive and responsible workers.

Of course, there still are corporate executives who don't believe that alcoholism is a treatable disease. Despite ever-increasing evidence that alcoholics do recover and resume careers as productive and responsible employees, some administrators are stuck in old perceptions. Many think that the saying "Once an alcoholic always an alcoholic" means that alcoholics can't change their ways. While it is true that science has not yet found a way to cure alcoholism permanently, this does not mean that the situation is hopeless. The disease cannot yet be cured, but it can be arrested. Several million alcoholics in various stages of sobriety are living testimony to the fact that alcoholics can lead productive, fulfilling, responsible, and sober lives. Many of these alcoholics will not relapse into active illness and destructive drinking. Moreover, it is often the case that the creativity and vision that organizations need come from the creative, sensitive, and gifted alcoholic employee.

But while corporations are beginning to do their part, it is equally important that we alcoholics shoulder some of the responsibility. Our companies, no matter how well meaning, cannot keep us sober, nor should we expect them to. In the final analysis, we may have a disease, but once we understand this fact, it is our responsibility to get into action, to take the necessary steps to maintain our sobriety. If a company program helps us to get and pay for treatment, then we should acknowledge our gratitude. It is unrealistic for some of us to expect companies to pay for our treatment again and again because we sober up only to return to drinking when we figure it is safe to do so. At some point, even the most reasonable company will have to draw the line and insist that its employees report for work ready, willing, and able to do a competent job in return for fair wages. In short, companies must have adequate job performance whether we are alcoholic or not.

Companies have obligations to their other employees as well. In many industrial settings where health and safety are constant and real concerns, intoxicated employees pose serious problems for coworkers. Alcoholic workers who handle dangerous chemicals and explosives, operate heavy equipment, and manage risky production processes simply must be sober on the job. Think about it for a minute. At 32,000 feet in the air, would you resent an airline for insisting that the pilot of your jumbo jet be cold sober at the controls? Imagine what it would be like to fly coast-to-coast in planes commanded by drinking pilots, guided by drunken air traffic controllers, and staffed by flight attendants staggering up and down the aisles with steaming pots of coffee in their hands. Or to take another example, picture yourself on the Lexington Avenue train in New York's subway system at rush hour. Talking about alcoholism on the job means talking about the operator of that rush-hour train stuffed to the windows with homeward-bound workers. Do we want this operator alert, responsible, and sober? Or are we foolish enough to insist that any possible drinking by this fellow is really his business and that he has a right to do as he pleases?

Talking about alcoholism at work may mean talking about our surgeons, psychiatrists, accountants, automobile mechanics, dentists, pediatricians, bus drivers, and oil burner repairmen. The man who is replacing our worn-out roofs may have his own opinions about the harmlessness of having a "couple of beers" on the job. So may the fellows who are taking down a towering old Norway maple tree that stands just fifteen feet from our front doors. All of us want the police officers who patrol our towns and cities with loaded pistols at the ready to be sober. We want those whose job it is to push or refrain from pushing the button that would start World War III to be very sober indeed.

Those of us who are alcoholics truly do need to keep one thing straight: alcoholism and the world of work do not mix. Too many people besides ourselves have a stake in how we perform our jobs.

According to Sigmund Freud, the father of psychoanalysis, life is mainly about love and work. While Dr. Freud may have been wrong about certain things, he was right on target here. Work is a big part of our lives. Often it is the most troubling and stressful part of our lives.

While a person's work does not cause his or her alcoholism, particular jobs can complicate recovery. A recovering alcoholic musician or bartender, for example, may find that nightclubs and bars just don't go with a sober lifestyle. Some people can do these jobs sober, but many cannot. The constant availability of alcohol, party atmospheres, and pressures to drink in these situations are factors that make continued recovery chancy indeed.

Of course, there are job aspects other than alcohol availability that might prove to be negative factors in recovery. There may be a mismatch between an alcoholic's personality characteristics and the demands of his job. A person who is truly comfortable only in the outdoors is probably going to fight a desk job long and hard. People who need warm, trusting, open, sincere, and supportive interpersonal relationships won't be happy in work organizations in which game playing, secrecy, competitiveness, guardedness, and political maneuvering are the norm. Some jobs may be just too stressful for anybody to be happy in them. Others may be far too dangerous. Still other jobs may force one to put one's values aside and to engage in shady, deceptive practices. In some organizational contexts, it is simply impossible to be yourself; the job requires you to keep your mouth shut, agree to everything, initiate nothing, to wear your organizational mask at all times.

Recovering alcoholics, after a reasonable period of sobriety, need to do an honest inventory of their skills, needs, and goals with regard to careers, occupations, and employment. This occupational inventory should not be considered until at least a year of sobriety has been achieved, and probably should be delayed in most cases until the beginning of the third or fourth years of sobriety. It is sometimes the case that job or career dissatisfaction diminishes as sobriety lengthens.

But for those stubborn cases of frustrating nonfulfillment at work that persist long into sobriety, we must be prepared to seek out new opportunities for ourselves and to plan effectively for career changes. Job changes may mean sacrifices in the form of temporary reductions in income, the challenge of further education and training, and the insecurity of mid-career shifts in direction. But if we are to be sober, and perhaps more importantly, *joyously sober*, then we may find it necessary to come to grips with the realities of careers, jobs, occupations, and professions.

As the famous serenity prayer states: "God, grant me the serenity to accept the things I cannot change, the courage to change the things I can, and the wisdom to know the difference."

Self-fulfillment and joyous realization of our potentials at work may require us to pursue the middle portion of this prayer in earnest: *God, grant me the courage to change the things I can.*

CHAPTER 10

What to Expect from Treatment

Not every alcoholic will need formal treatment in order to recover from alcoholism. Many are able to get sober and stay that way through Alcoholics Anonymous alone. Some may find a way out of the disease through still other means. But many people will need treatment of some kind or another if their sobriety is to be achieved and maintained. For these alcoholics who do need alcoholism treatment, some basic understanding of this relatively new and specialized treatment approach is in order.

Alcoholics, of course, do not relish going into treatment. No alcoholic to my knowledge has ever said anything like the following: "Well, it's a wonderful day today. My wife loves me. My kids adore me. I'm making a lot of money. The neighbors think I'm a swell guy and everybody at work lets me know that the place would fall apart without me. I'm usually happy, satisfied, contented with my life, and positive about my future. I guess I'll run down to the local alcoholism treatment center and get a little treatment!"

Usually, there are pressures of some kind or another in the life of the alcoholic that are pushing him toward treatment. The pressures may be external, internal, or a combination of the two. External pressures may involve family, friends, lovers, police, courts, judges, lawyers, and employers.

A showdown in the family where the spouse has given what looks very much like an ultimatum may be a motivating factor for some alcoholics.

These ultimatums take various forms but the bottom line is "get help or get out!" Threats, however, are serious business and spouses of alcoholics should think deeply and carefully before using these. *As a rule, spouses should not make threats unless they fully intend to carry them out.* Spouses should also be aware that ultimatums with alcoholics more often fail than succeed in producing the desired results.

An arrest for drunken driving, assault and battery, or other trouble with the law after drinking may bring us into conflict with the police. Family quarrels that get out of hand may do the same. In these cases, alcoholics may find themselves heading for treatment not under the press of their own inner motives, but at the suggestion of some knowing judge.

Alcoholism programs at work have started many alcoholics on the road to recovery since fear of loss of livelihood does affect alcoholics considerably. By focussing on deteriorating job performance, supervisors and bosses were informed and caring enough to make interventions into the lives of employees and probably saved their lives. Physicians knowledgeable about alcoholism have helped some of us to see the devastating impact of chronic, heavy drinking on our bodies. Traumatic injuries sustained in accidents during drinking bouts gave many of us pause.

Some alcoholics, as AA members so aptly put it, just became sick and tired of being sick and tired! They dragged themselves into an AA meeting or a treatment center simply because something had to be better than what they had. The fear, remorse, guilt, and pain of their drinking had created *internal* pressures too troublesome to ignore or deny further.

In recent years, formal interventions involving the alcoholic and a group of concerned persons whose lives are attached to him can be arranged. Members of the family, friends, and perhaps even employers are first trained by experts on how to collect their observations of the alcoholic. They learn to put these into useable form and then to share them effectively and sensitively with the alcoholic at an appropriate time. When all members of this intervention team have been instructed and trained, a group meeting with the alcoholic is arranged. Under the guidance of the intervention expert, each member of the group shares his observations with the alcoholic. These observations are not vague, highly general statements, but short, concise, and accurate accounts of the alcoholic's behavior on specific occasions. For example, the spouse may say something like the following: "When we went to Hawaii for our tenth wedding anniversary, you were drunk before we got on the plane, slept from Los Angeles to Hilo, woke up with a hangover when we hit the runway, had a couple in the airport bar, and then started up again at dinner. For one whole week, you never drew a sober breath. I was alternately ashamed, angry, disappointed, frustrated, and finally crazy with fear over what would become of us."

An adult child of an alcoholic might say something like: "The night I graduated from high school, you decided not to come home directly from work but to stop off at a bar. I was ashamed that you didn't make it to my graduation, but even more ashamed when you showed up later drunk at the party at our house. I was mortified to have my friends see you in such a state. When they all made excuses and left early for other parties, I was really crushed. Daddy, I really love you. I do, I do. I want you to know that. But I want you to get help for yourself too."

Formal interventions, if conducted sensitively and carefully by a well-trained intervention specialist, are very effective in motivating more and more alcoholics into treatment. Such interventions, however, should not be tried by families and friends without an expert guide. And the emphasis must be on a loving, caring, and sensitive intervention that centers upon the actual past behavior of the alcoholic and the need for treatment.

Once an alcoholic accepts the need for treatment, what happens then? Treatment of any kind usually begins with a complete medical history, physical examination, and, if necessary, detoxification. The medical examination will have a number of purposes. The first purpose is to assess the patient's current condition so that detoxification can be planned intelligently. Detoxification is the technical term for the procedures through which alcohol is withdrawn from the person in a safe manner. It may or may not involve the use of medication. Some alcoholics can get through the first few days of stopping drinking with nothing more than a calm, stable social environment with lots of support, caring, reassurance, and understanding. Others will need medications to control withdrawal symptoms such as rapid pulse, elevated blood pressure, shakes, nervousness, agitation, and insomnia. Medications called benzodiazepines (Valium, Librium) are most often used in alcohol detoxification since these drugs are cross-tolerant with alcohol (see Chapter 8). These medications are given in gradually decreasing doses over several days until withdrawal symptoms are no longer a threat.

Medical staff will need to find out if other drugs have been used along with alcohol; how much the patient has been drinking and for how long; if there is a history of convulsions during alcohol withdrawal; what allergies and drug sensitivities there might be; and if there are special medical problems. Pulse rate, blood pressure, and body temperature will be measured to see if vital signs are normal or if serious withdrawal symptoms are imminent.

Usually, the examining physician, physician's assistant, or nurse practitioner will see that a standard battery of laboratory tests are ordered. These may include blood chemistry analyses, urinalysis, electrocardiogram, and chest films when indicated. Some physicians will want a complete nutritional assessment as well to determine if possible neglect of diet during the drinking years has led to nutritional imbalances and deficiencies of various kinds.

Although used to detect diseases, laboratory tests ordered by the physician may often also point to a diagnosis of alcoholism. See the table below for some tests useful in a diagnosis of alcoholism. Various profiles combining these tests have been found to be useful in diagnosing alcoholism by researchers at the National Institute on Alcohol Abuse and Alcoholism. In fact, certain profiles taken from just ten of these laboratory tests accurately identified 98 percent of the alcoholics in a sample and 100 percent of the nonalcoholics.

Test	Low to High Normal Values	Description of Test
MCV	80 - 100	Size of red blood cells
Sodium	136 - 145	Level of sodium in serum
Phosphorus	2.5 - 4.2	Level of phosphorus in serum
Bun	6 - 26	Blood urea nitrogen
Chloride	96 - 108	Level of chloride in serum
Carbon dioxide	22 - 31	Level of gas in blood
SGPT	0 - 45	Liver function
SGOT	0 - 41	Liver function
GGTP	6 - 53	Liver function
LDH	60 - 245	Liver function
Alkaline phosphatase	30 - 115	Liver function
Triglycerides	30 - 175	Blood fat
Total bilirubin	0.2 - 1.2	Predominant yellow pigment of bile

Lab tests, however, are used mainly to detect various diseases that alcoholics may have. For example, the liver function tests are useful in discovering alcohol-related damage to the liver. They can also help the physician to uncover other liver diseases such as infectious hepatitis. Blood glucose (sugar) is a concern because of possible diabetes, or high blood sugar. Low blood sugar, or *hypoglycemia*, may also be of interest to the physician. When the blood sugar falls to low levels, the person may feel faint, dizzy, irritable, depressed, tired, and emotionally unstable.

While blood sugar level does drop in the course of a bout of heavy drinking, experts do not agree that alcoholics suffer from a condition called "functional hypoglycemia" that *persists into recovery*. Some specialists in alcoholism treatment boldly assert that *all* alcoholics have hypoglycemia and should eat special high protein – low carbohydrate diets in order to prevent sudden drops in blood sugar several hours after eating. Other specialists do not think the scientific evidence favors such an extreme position.

Depending on how it is done and interpreted, a test called a *five hour glucose tolerance test* may or may not confirm a diagnosis of hypoglycemia. This test involves taking a blood sample every hour for five hours after an initial oral dose of a syrup laced with sugar. If the blood sugar falls to a very low level at the later hours, some physicians feel hypoglycemia is present. This fall in blood sugar is thought to be due to a massive insulin release. In effect, the hypoglycemic cannot eat simple carbohydrates because these signal the adrenals to release too much insulin. This hyperinsulin response supposedly drives the sugar level in the blood far too low. If a person is convinced they have the illness despite a negative five hour glucose tolerance test, they might try having their blood sugar tested at the time their symptoms are taking place. Often, this method of testing reveals that the patient's symptoms are not caused by low blood sugar after all. The symptoms that the person is experiencing may be warning signs of possible serious diseases other than hypoglycemia. These possibilities should be explored thoroughly by a physician.

Aside from difficulties in getting a reliable diagnosis of hypoglycemia, treatment with a high protein – low carbohydrate diet may not be without risks. Persons with cholesterol and fat problems may have trouble with these diets because much of the dietary protein is derived from eggs, dairy, and red meat. Perhaps most important, the oxidation of alcohol produces striking metabolic imbalances in the liver. Increased production of uric acid coupled with decreased capacity of the kidneys to excrete uric acid may aggravate or trigger off attacks of *gout*. Alcoholics with severe liver damage from drinking should not be advised to eat high protein diets, nor should persons suffering from kidney diseases or who have histories of gout.

Finally, recent findings suggest that *food allergy* may be the underlying condition that triggers hypoglycemia. Drs. H.L. Newbold, Marshall Mandell, and William Philpott have independently discussed the curious findings that foods other than simple carbohydrates can produce rapid falls in blood sugar level. This, of course, is completely contrary to the traditional view of functional hypoglycemia in which a problem with the insulin response to simple carbohydrates is assumed to be primary. In effect, it may be that allergy is the main problem in hypoglycemia and not excessive insulin production in response to simple carbohydrates.

In short, hypoglycemia, nutrition, and diet are issues in the recovery of alcoholics that require expert medical diagnosis and guidance by properly trained nutritionists. When such expert care is sought, the person may discover that he is not hypoglycemic. Moreover, even when there is strong suspicion that hypoglycemia does exist, a diet rich in *complex carbohydrates* and *low in protein* may be the diet of choice. Many nutritionists now feel that the normal American diet is far too rich in protein.

Although there are exceptions, *high fiber, high complex carbohydrate, low fat, and low protein diets may be far more appropriate for most people, including those who suffer from various disturbances related to eating products made from refined sugars.*

The issue of hypoglycemia may be more complex than previously realized, but one nutrition fact remains clear: *alcoholics need to eat nourishing and balanced meals both during their drinking years and during recovery.* Alcohol as a food is grossly inadequate. It consists almost entirely of empty calories. In each gram of ethyl alcohol there are seven calories and virtually no protein, vitamins or minerals.

Not only does alcohol clog the diet with empty calories, it has a direct negative impact on nutrition. Because of the effects of alcohol on the intestine, there is poor absorption of vitamins, minerals, and other nutrients. Damage to the liver may affect metabolism and glucose storage. Potassium and magnesium may be lost from the body in excess amounts. Calcium may be removed from the bones. Low levels of these minerals can lead to various rhythmic disturbances of the heart.

Because of these nutritional problems, alcoholics should be counseled by properly trained nutritionists to eat properly. Along with other addicted people, alcoholics should be advised to stay away from excessive amounts of caffeine either in coffee or in sodas. Because of possible "rebound" reactions to excessive sugar consumption, candy, cakes, sodas, and other forms of "junk foods" should be avoided. One does not have to suffer from hypoglycemia *per se* to feel weak, depressed, and irritable several hours after eating a lot of refined sugar products. Since alcoholics need to reach balanced emotional states as soon as possible in recovery, they should eat diets that promote balance rather than extreme highs and lows in energy and mood. After five cups of strong coffee, even nonalcoholics would like a drink or two to calm them down!

As far as vitamin and mineral supplementation go, a multi-vitamin tablet that meets National Research Council recommended daily dietary allowances should be sufficient for many alcoholics. However, those alcoholics who suffer from serious deficiencies should seek treatment from a qualified health care professional. Since treating oneself with very high doses of vitamins and minerals can be dangerous, alcoholics should not attempt megavitamin and mineral supplementations except under the care of a physician.

Physicians working in the field of alcoholism will usually order a chest film if a recent one is not available. Chest X-rays are important because heavy smoking and alcoholism seem to go hand in hand. *Alcoholics are surely addicted to the nicotine in cigarette smoke, but they may also be addicted to the acetaldehyde that is also present in cigarette smoke.* Acetaldehyde is the first metabolic breakdown product of alcohol (see Chapter 4). In other words, when we drink alcohol, enzymes in our bodies go to work on the alcohol, and it is first metabolized to an intermediate product called acetaldehyde. Acetaldehyde is a toxic and addictive substance in its own right, and it is found in cigarette smoke. This may explain why the smoking of alcoholics goes up when they first quit drinking. The small quantities of acetaldehyde in cigarette smoke may be even more important to recovering alcoholics in the absence of both the alcohol and the acetaldehyde formed from it by the body.

But to return to the main point, the compulsive smoking of most alcoholics results in lung damage, and perhaps more serious diseases like emphysema and cancer. Among younger alcoholics who smoke marijuana, physicians will probably order chest films because of the early destructive lung changes doctors have been seeing in young marijuana smokers. While both are bad, marijuana smoking is far more damaging to the lungs than is cigarette smoke. Experts state that several marijuana cigarettes a day are equal to about a pack of cigarettes.

Tests for tuberculosis, cardiac problems, thyroid malfunction, neurological disorders, mental illness and other diseases are done if suspicion exists that the patient may have these problems. Alcoholism, in later stages, can attack virtually every organ of the human body and produce serious diseases. It is important to realize, however, that "later stages" does not mean "old." Serious alcohol-related diseases are sometimes seen in seventeen-year-olds and are often seen in young adults in their early twenties.

If serious problems other than alcoholism are detected, they of course must be managed. Where appropriate, simultaneous treatment in the alcoholism treatment center will be started. In some cases, the patient will have to be referred to a specialist or general medical setting to have the problem dealt with before alcoholism treatment can be continued.

For various psychiatric disturbances such as severe depression, panic disorders, manic-depressive illnesses, and psychotic reactions, individualized treatments with both psychotherapy and medications will be necessary. If the psychiatric condition is severe enough, transfer to an appropriate facility will be necessary. *The large majority of alcoholics, however, are not mentally ill and will not require either general psychiatric treatments or long-term psychoactive medications in order to recover.* Alcoholism treatment is not psychiatric treatment, and alcoholism treatment facilities are not psychiatric treatment centers.

When people are going into alcoholism treatment, they are often frightened about what they might find. Are the other patients crazy? Are the other patients deep into delirium tremens (the DTs)? Do they see bugs crawling all over them, bats, snakes, and roaches? Are they falling down with convulsions? Are they violent?

These fears are not realistic; very few patients in an alcoholism treatment center show such extreme behaviors during withdrawal and detoxification. With modern medical treatments, delirium tremens are quite rare; most modern alcoholism treatment centers see only a few of these cases a year. Convulsions are also no longer common. They do occur, but at much lower rate now that effective medications such as Valium, Librium, and Dilantin are available. As for violence, treatment center staffs will not permit such behavior from patients. If a patient makes violent threats or begins to act violently, he is usually transferred promptly to a type of treatment facility that is prepared to deal with more extreme behavior.

Modern alcoholism treatment centers are not "snake pits." Most are attractive, cheerful, pleasant, clean, nicely furnished, and professionally managed facilities. Staffs are well-trained in their specialties and know how to work with alcoholic patients and their families. For the most part, alcoholism treatment centers are not "locked wards." The typical center is an open facility and patients may leave treatment if they decide to do so.

Once the medical aspects of early treatment are completed, the focus shifts from body to mind. Counseling, either in outpatient or inpatient settings, is the mainstay of treatment. In one-to-one sessions with an alcoholism counselor, psychologist, or other trained professional, the patient begins the long and often arduous task of finding out who he is and what alcoholism has done to him. These individual sessions are usually the place for discussion of material too sensitive to bring up in other settings.

In group therapy sessions, the patient has the chance to hear stories from other alcoholics, to find out how they are coping with their illnesses, and how they are approaching recovery. Groups permit the alcoholic to identify, to see himself in the life stories of other people. In the group, he understands that he is not alone, that others have suffered as he has, and that he wasn't the only one to do unpredictable and odd things while drinking. These learnings from group therapy help the alcoholic to understand that he is not as different from others as he imagined. He discovers that others have done many of the things he has. He feels less guilty and he starts learning to laugh at some of the actions that prior to treatment made him feel so ashamed that he kept returning to drink to quiet his guilt and remorse.

Group therapy permits the alcoholic to find out about his own feelings as well as those of others. He learns to recognize and accept his anger rather than to let it explode over the wrong things and at the wrong people. He also learns that he has tender feelings too. Many alcoholics discover in group therapy settings that, along with their anger, there is a great deal of love in them as well. Frustration, grief, sorrow, and loss are talked about openly as patients explore the myriad ways that alcoholism has complicated their relationships, shattered their dreams, and, in some cases, destroyed their careers. *Feelings are not the cause of alcoholism. However, they can be triggers that start a drinking bout.* As such, they have to be recognized and managed by alcoholics who wish to stay sober.

Group settings also permit people to share recovery plans. Practical issues such as the following are discussed thoroughly: How does an alcoholic turn down the offer of a drink? Should alcoholics keep alcoholic beverages around? Does switching from scotch to beer help? How do we handle negative emotional states such as depression, fear, and anger? What can an alcoholic do when craving for a drink seizes him? Can we alcoholics go to parties where drinks are served? These are but a few of the many questions that get discussed in group settings.

Lectures are a very important part of alcoholism treatment today. Most treatment centers have daily lectures on subjects such as how alcohol affects the body and why addiction is really a disease. Lectures can also cover things like the signs and symptoms of alcoholism, the costs of the disease to ourselves and society, alcoholism and the family, and so forth.

Individual counseling, group therapy, and the lectures have one critical overarching goal: *to help alcoholics to break through the protective wall of defenses and to see their disease clearly and realistically.* Treatment is but the beginning of recovery. However, it is an important beginning. If the alcoholic comes out of treatment knowing more about his illness, aware of his defenses, and committed to staying sober, treatment will have done its job well.

Some people—including certain professionals—believe that alcoholics need not stay sober in order to recover. They believe that alcoholism is not a disease and that alcoholics can learn to control their drinking, reduce it to normal limits, and keep on drinking without suffering the problems which usually follow in the wake of active alcoholism. *In effect, these advocates of controlled drinking are claiming that alcoholism can be cured, not merely arrested as most experts in the field believe.*

The possibility of controlled or "nonproblem drinking" as a realistic treatment goal for alcoholics is, of course, a most serious issue. Many alcoholics have died, killed other people, ruined their lives through accidents, or destroyed their social reputations trying to prove that they could drink like the nonalcoholics of the world do. Drinking alcoholics want to believe in the possibility of controlled drinking. Given the right spouse, lover, job, or set of circumstances, they might just be able to pull it off—have a couple of drinks a night and let it go at that! This delusion is the fundamental delusion of the disease. Perhaps the saddest sight there is to see is the alcoholic lying in a hospital bed dying of cirrhosis of the liver, while proclaiming that he doesn't have a disease called alcoholism and that he can "handle his booze."

The scientific evidence for controlled drinking among alcoholics is meager, flimsy, shoddy, unimpressive, and highly controversial. The major studies that claimed to find evidence of controlled drinking among alcoholics have been discredited. For example, the 1976 Rand Corporation study of eight federally funded alcoholism treatment centers that made the front pages of the *New York Times* and purported to find large numbers of controlled drinking alcoholics was little more than statistical nonsense. The Rand study samples were riddled with bias due to the loss of far too many subjects. Moreover, the measurements of controlled drinking were not valid and covered only thirty days' worth of drinking. In a later study reported in 1980, the Rand authors (two social scientists and one psychologist) found that controlled drinking could not be sustained over longer periods of time.

Another major study, by psychologists Mark and Linda Sobell, conducted in the early 1970s at Patton State Hospital in California received much professional praise (from other psychologists) and great attention from the media. While the Sobells claimed to find that the patients trained to control their drinking in treatment functioned better during follow-up than patients given abstention treatment, other independent investigators have not supported these claims. Some years later, psychologists Mary Pendery and Irving Maltzman along with psychiatrist J. West re-interviewed the twenty patients who had received controlled drinking treatment from the Sobells. While the Sobells had presented findings that seemed to show that nineteen out of twenty of these patients were functioning well after treatment, the Pendery and Maltzman findings on these patients told a much different story. Nineteen of the twenty subjects had quickly relapsed back into active alcoholism and showed the typical negative personal, medical, and social consequences that go with drinking among alcoholics.

There are, of course, numerous papers other than those by the Rand

Corporation authors and the Sobells that claimed to find evidence of controlled drinking among alcoholics. For the most part, however, inspection of these papers reveals that they too are highly suspect on technical, scientific grounds. Moreover, where some success is apparent, it is clear that these successes have been achieved with problem drinkers or occasional alcohol abusers, and not with alcoholics. In fact, one psychologist heavily involved in controlled drinking research, Dr. William Miller, makes it a point to refer alcoholics to AA or to abstention-oriented treatment programs.

Controlled drinking for alcoholics is not a new idea. It was dreamed up by alcoholics themselves long before behavioristically-oriented psychologists and psychiatrists hit upon the notion. In fact, ask any recovering alcoholic now committed to a program of complete sobriety what methods of controlling his drinking he tried before surrendering to the fact that he couldn't. Chances are good that he will come up with a list that includes all of the methods that behavioristic psychologists have stumbled upon, and more! Unfortunately, while many of these tricks seemed to work in the short run, in the long run they were little more than temporary (but dangerous) detours on the road to complete and total sobriety.

Controlled drinking for alcoholics isn't a bad idea. It's simply a wrong idea. In the long run, it doesn't work. Alcoholics don't get well by drinking alcohol. They get well by not drinking alcohol. As the old saying goes, "If you don't drink alcohol, you can't get drunk." This simple observation seems to be over the heads of some of our more sophisticated thinkers in the social and behavioral sciences.

Much of alcoholism treatment will focus upon the typical defenses that alcoholics use to protect their drinking and their self-esteem while drinking. Denial is an important defense that must come apart in treatment, the alcoholic's automatic tendency to "cover up." Alcoholics often don't want to look at the reality of their drinking, see the results of it, or listen to somebody who is trying to help them.

There are many forms of denial: refusing to admit to drinking; distorting the quantity of drinking; denying that the drinking is causing problems; believing that we don't need help with the problem; denying that we are alcoholics. These are all variants of denial.

Rationalization, the act of making our drinking appear reasonable to ourselves and others, is another defense used by alcoholics. Minimizing is a further defense. Through minimization, the alcoholic persists in trying to reduce the severity of his problem. Rationalization takes the form of "I drink because. . ." while minimization usually goes something like "My drinking isn't so bad, look at Harry's!"

All of these defenses that alcoholics use are primary targets of early treatment. If the alcoholic is to get well, cracks in this armoring against the truth must begin to appear. The manner in which these cracks are made to happen, however, is an important issue. While attempting to find out the truth about themselves, alcoholics will need much love and support along with a firm push toward reality.

Learning to relax and have fun are a big part of recovery from alcoholism. Many alcoholics simply have never learned to play. Tense, driving, and success-oriented, many routinely pushed themselves beyond their limits. Alcohol or tranquilizers were used to calm down a racing mind and body.

Many treatment centers provide formal instruction in relaxation techniques. Meditation, use of biofeedback machines, stress management training, and relaxation training are often taught to combat the high levels of tension, stress, and anxiety alcoholics show. The purpose is to teach the alcoholic how to become aware of increasing stress and tension, and what to do to bring these unpleasant states back to normal without resorting to alcohol or other chemicals.

Modern treatment usually provides family therapy too. In well-designed family programs, spouses and other concerned persons have the opportunity to get help for themselves first of all. The stress of living near active alcoholism typically results in problems of some kind or another. Group treatment of family members along with members of other families usually provides great benefits. It is comforting for family members to discover that it isn't all their fault, that they didn't cause the alcoholic's drinking, and that they have done nothing for which they deserved punishment. Learning more about alcoholism as a disease, how it affects thinking and behavior, and what can be done about it often helps. Group treatment of family members gives them a safe context in which to dump the heavy load of anger, grief, sorrow, and resentment they have been carrying, often for years.

In some cases, *couples therapy* in which husband and wife look at their problems either alone or with other couples is tried. In other cases, entire families are treated together in *family systems therapy*.

Which form of family treatment is needed is determined by a host of things. If the alcoholic family has literally reorganized in response to the disease, then whole family systems therapy may be absolutely necessary. Family reorganization takes place when important functions and roles are redistributed among family members. When the wife becomes the major breadwinner, pays the bills, makes all the financial decisions, manages the household, cleans, and cooks, a major reorganization of the family has taken place. If the husband does all of these things in response to alcoholism in a wife, then the family has reorganized. Children may take over the functions and roles of a severely dysfunctional parent. It is not unusual to find "ten-year-old mothers" who have picked up the duties, obligations, and adult characteristics of wives and mothers.

Treatment of the family is usually designed to help alcoholic families hold up a mirror to themselves, to see themselves as they are as a unit, and to begin to understand the strong feelings of anger, shame, guilt, and hopelessness into which alcoholism has plunged them. Learning to share feelings, to communicate wants and needs directly, and to change destructive behavior patterns are critical goals of family treatment. Treatment should help the family to see that a further reorganization of the family may be necessary if a healthy pattern of roles, functions, and relationships is to be brought about. Seeing the need for this new reorganization and bringing it about, however, are very different things. Roles once established are tough to change. Spouses may be uneasy with turning certain responsibilities over to the recovering alcoholic. Children may actually resent the return of a strong and interested father or mother to the fold. In the drinking days, they may have had the freedom of neglect as well as the pain of it. Now that the parent as disciplinarian is once again in their lives, they may rebel.

Sexual love and relationships between husband and wife may require expert guidance to return to normal. Alcohol in large doses can cause the testicles to malfunction. As a result, there may be sharp decrease in testosterone, the male sex hormone. Lowered sex drive, impotence, premature ejaculation, inability to orgasm, and other problems may have plagued the marriage. But it isn't all physical. Resentments, anger, depression, and shame can wreck havoc on marital sex. As the alcoholism progressed, spouses were turned off by the increasing unattractiveness of their mates. Of course, many of these sexual problems cannot be dealt with in early alcoholism treatment. *Often, alcoholic couples will have to wait for a period of sobriety to be achieved before these more complex problems can be treated by a specialist.* In early treatment, however, the alcoholic patient can become aware of these problems and make plans for their treatment later on if necessary.

The concepts of Alcoholics Anonymous are a major aspect of modern alcoholism treatment. These concepts may be learned through staff lectures, readings, and attendance at AA meetings while in treatment. Spiritual growth (not religious affiliation) as achieved through the steps of the AA program should be started through work with specialized alcoholism counselors. Alcoholics in treatment owe it to themselves to give AA a chance while they are in treatment and also when they return to their communities. Spouses of alcoholics, older children, and other significant persons should plan to attend Al-Anon meetings while their mates, parents, or friends are in treatment and after they leave treatment. These self-help programs are not for everybody who needs them, but for those who want them. As a consequence, AA, Al-Anon and Alateen probably won't be useful for everybody. But everybody should at least give them a try.

The final ingredient of treatment is *aftercare* planning for continuing therapy. The recovery from alcoholism will not be finished in thirty days, sixty days, or even a year. Recovery is a lifelong process that begins with early treatment, continues into aftercare, and then becomes a self-directed activity for life. Plans for formal aftercare need to be devised while the patient is in treatment, and some attention should be given to what the patient will do when several months have passed and formal aftercare ends. One of the marvelous things about Alcoholics Anonymous and Al-Anon is simply that these programs will always be there and they are free. As far as long-term recovery programs go, it is difficult to imagine a better bargain than AA, Al-Anon, and Alateen.

In summarizing what alcoholics should expect from treatment, the following checklist might be helpful. Any reasonably good alcoholism treatment center should provide the following:

1. Complete and total abstention from alcohol should be the treatment goal (a little bit of controlled or moderate drinking is not a realistic goal of alcoholism treatment). Except for brief use of medication in detoxification and specialized treatment of certain psychiatric patients, drugs are not a part of the treatment program;
2. Physical assessments that include a physical examination, routine blood chemistries and urinalysis, EKG, and chest films when indicated should be done on all patients;
3. Medical detoxification should be available and can be used if needed;
4. Adequate professional staff including physicians, nurses, physician assistants, psychologists, psychiatrists, alcoholism counselors, social workers, clergy, and recreational counselors should be available in sufficient numbers;
5. Individual and group treatments should be provided;
6. The concepts of AA should be available for learning either formally or informally through in-house AA meetings;
7. Aftercare planning and programs should be an integral part of treatment;
8. The facility should be attractive, cheerful, well-furnished, and comfortable. Meals should be nutritious, appetizing, and served in friendly, clean, and warm environments;
9. An educational program consisting of lectures, films, books, pamphlets, and papers should be employed;

10. Individual treatment planning should be done routinely and treatment plan reviews held; individualized treatments should be available;
11. There should be an adequate family program;
12. The center should be professionally managed and administered by staffs competent in health care administration.

While many alcoholics approach the need for treatment with doubts and suspicions of the worst, their fears are usually groundless. Most patients find treatment to be an exciting and fulfilling experience. For the first time in their lives, they find out that they can face their disease honestly and squarely with very positive results. The results are often amazing.

In treatment, alcoholics can finally learn what the disease of alcoholism is all about. And if they work at it, they can begin to find out what they are all about too. Alcoholism is indeed a disease of the body to which we are made susceptible by our genetic histories and by the chemistries of our brains. However, this disease of the body cannot be activated if we don't drink alcohol. What we must do is learn enough about ourselves that we can neutralize our various psychological triggers before they lead to the drink that leads to a drunk that leads to the biochemical trap of active alcoholism.

Perhaps more important than knowledge, we may find from treatment that it is possible to *feel good* without alcohol or drugs in our bodies. With renewed respect for ourselves, appreciation of our strengths and limitations, and awareness of the needs of others, we may find our worlds easier and friendlier than we ever imagined they could be.

CHAPTER 11

The Reality Principle: Surrender Sets Us Free

If we were to immerse ourselves in the media of our times, we would quickly come to the conclusion that modern human beings are obsessed with power. The reports from the sports arenas of the world inform us that the competitive spirit is often less about individual mastery than it is about the domination of one human being over another. Fantasies about the rich and the powerful attract us while the realities of the lives of the poor and less influential go unnoticed. In our corporations, universities, hospitals, and other public and private organizations, the struggle to get to the top of the heap is incessant. And the steady stream of images from the various battlefields of the world reminds us that the never-ending wars of humankind are becoming more cruel and devastating as the armies grow larger, the bombs multiply, and the weapons of destruction permit more deadly aim.

In all of these images of the serious business of humankind, the message is clear: it is good to be powerful and no good at all to be powerless. The powerful are constantly the subject of the evening news. The powerless get no coverage at all, except perhaps as victims.

Is it any wonder then that we find it difficult to admit to being anything other than complete masters of ourselves? And are we not secretly suspicious of the person who doesn't care about achieving a position of influence and power over others? Not only do we live in a world in which power is adored and powerlessness scorned, many of us are raised from childhood on to seek power as the means to further ourselves, often at the expense of others. Some of us learn to seek power as an end in and of itself, a worthy goal to pursue regardless of the costs to ourselves and to others around us. Power neurotics are much in evidence in our modern work organizations, many rising to the upper reaches where they must compulsively control, dominate, and prevail over all contrary opinion and wishes. In such organizations, one must think as the boss does and do what the boss wants. The message is once again clear: power is right and there is no truth in powerlessness.

These thoughts on power are of more than philosophical interest in alcoholism. Consider the drinking alcoholic and his plight. The facts of his disease are steadily accumulating. In his wake, there may be a trail of broken promises and relationships. There may be humiliations almost too painful for him to bear. He may have suffered the terrible shock of complete rejection by friends, lovers, or family. His body may be deteriorating steadily from the toxic effects of alcohol. His mind is not as sharp as it used to be. There is the sickening ache of loneliness, emptiness, and isolation in his soul. Yet he must continue to drink alcohol, for to stop would be an admission that he cannot control himself. How can he admit to powerlessness when the world as he understands it demands that he be in control of himself, his life, and his destiny? In the world as the alcoholic imagines it to be, there are only winners and losers. And who wants to be a loser?

For many alcoholics, the refusal to recognize what alcohol has done to them is almost automatic. Recognition of the effects of alcohol on their lives would require action, but to take action would, in turn, imply powerlessness. This is quite a knot. To get well, you must first recognize that you are ill. But if you recognize that you are ill, this means you must take the necessary, responsible steps to deal with your illness. But if you take these necessary, responsible steps, this proves that you are indeed ill. And you don't want to be ill because *this* illness not only reflects upon your character but demands that you stop doing whatever it is you were doing that made you ill in the first place. To make things even worse, suppose you happen not only to like what you have been doing but have literally built your life around it. This is a knot indeed!

Many drinking alcoholics never manage to deal with this particular dilemma. Those of us who manage to untie this knot understand that there is a paradox here, a seeming contradiction in all that we may have believed: *In order to win you must first surrender.*

In the war against alcoholism, we must not listen to counsel that urges us to stiffen our resolve, exert our will power, and fight back with all the strength we can muster. As reasonable as such advice might appear, it usually results in a humiliating and crushing defeat at the hands of our more powerful adversary.

Nor should we place much faith in well-meaning advice to leave the field temporarily, to return later to renew our struggle. If we are alcoholic, giving up alcohol on a temporary basis—with the intention of going back to it as soon as our bodies will permit another bout—won't help very much. The trouble with "going on the wagon," giving up alcohol temporarily, is simply that most people end up "falling off the wagon" as readily as they got on.

Some people (including a small number of psychiatrists, psychologists, and other professionals) apparently believe that alcoholics need not abstain entirely from alcoholic beverages in order to recover. According to such minority opinion, alcoholics could control their drinking if they really wanted to, or they could be taught to control it. There is precious little acceptable scientific evidence to support these incautious claims concerning the feasibility of controlled drinking for the vast majority of alcoholics. Recent much-publicized studies purporting to find sustained controlled drinking in large percentages of the alcoholics studied have been thoroughly disproved. In effect, for alcoholics, there is little hope in the possibility of recovery if the drinking continues. To believe otherwise is to place our faith in fantasy and not fact.

As experience has shown, surrender cannot be an half-hearted attempt. We alcoholics must give up totally and without reservation if we hope to have any real chance of recovery from this potentially fatal disease. We must surrender completely to the obvious: *we can no longer exercise choice with regard to alcohol, and our personal and social affairs are beyond our control. We must accept the simple fact that we can no longer drink alcohol.*

This admission is, of course, a bitter pill to swallow. Typically, we want to fly in the face of reality, distort or deny the facts of our drinking and its consequences, and keep alive the fiction that there must be some mistake. We know alcoholics. We've watched *them* drink and we know we don't drink like *that*. In the world of active alcoholism, if we want to "prove" that we are not real alcoholics, we can always point at somebody whose drinking is clearly worse than our own. Comparing our drinking to the man or woman who has reached the end of the road of alcoholism is one way many of us delay the inevitable confrontation with ourselves and our own problematic drinking.

We try many other ways to avoid the painful recognition of the truth about ourselves and what we must do about our drinking. Blaming others is a common tactic we use to avoid complete surrender. Our wives or husbands are at fault for our drinking. If our children had turned out better we would not drink as we do. It is our parents, jobs, bosses, friends, lovers, communities, societies, and maybe even this miserable world that causes us to drink destructively. The implication here is that if other people would behave correctly, then we would be able to drink normally.

Because we have incorrectly diagnosed our problem, we may show a variety of inadequate attempts at solution. We may change jobs, move to other communities, divorce a spouse, take up a new career, buy a new house, get rid of our friends, and so forth. In effect, we will set about to change our lives in every way but the critical one. Everything must go or change except our drinking.

We alcoholics are often gifted in the art of rationalization. If all else fails, we can always rationalize our behavior, i.e., make it appear eminently reasonable to ourselves and to others. We drink because we are sensitive people in an insensitive world. Because we need it to relax. Because our careers were cut short by an unfortunate twist of fate. Because we have lost a fortune. Because we have gained a fortune. Because we need it to be creative, witty, charming, personable, and fun to be with. Because. Because. Because. *The excuses of alcoholism are endless.*

Rationalizations, however, simply permit us to dig the pit of alcoholism deeper. Given enough of these self-deceptions, many of us never do manage to climb back out. Those who do make it back from the hell of alcoholism know that while there are many excuses for an alcoholic to pick up a drink, there are no *valid reasons* to do so.

There are many other ways for us to avoid admitting to ourselves that there is no way out of the grip of alcoholism but to surrender. We can seek out friends who will tell us that it is only our imaginations, that we surely could not be alcoholics. The friends we choose for this "objective" opinion are often our drinking companions, people with whom we may have drunk ourselves into various states of intoxication many times before. We may deliberately choose professionals who do not specialize in alcoholism and who can be misled easily as to the true nature of our problems. For example, we may choose a physician who isn't likely to question our drinking practices too closely or resist our demands for tranquilizers too strongly. Avoiding psychologists and psychiatrists who are knowledgeable about alcoholism, we will find those who will endlessly analyze our social and emotional problems without ever connecting them to our destructive drinking. The measures alcoholics will take to avoid the final confrontation with self are simply astonishing.

But despite all of this fast and loose playing with the truth that we alcoholics do, the fact remains that many of us manage to recover. Even the least aware of us receive by grace moments of clarity in which our true conditions are revealed to us.

If we are to get well, we must first recognize the connection between drinking and the problems that have occurred and are continuing to occur in our lives. In trying to find out these facts about our drinking and our problems, it is often helpful to do a drinking inventory. Take a piece of paper and a pencil, choose a quiet spot where you won't be interrupted, and trace your drinking and its consequences over time. Write down the first drink you can remember. How old were you at the time? What situation were you in? What happened? Take the next drinking occasion you can remember and write down your age, the situation, and the consequences. Take larger intervals of time and mark down the trends of your drinking over these periods and the results of it. Do this from your earliest drinking to the present.

If you are completely honest with yourself, this drinking inventory will reveal to you the true extent to which alcohol has influenced your life. A pattern of negative consequences following drinking should become readily apparent to you if you are an alcoholic and are totally honest.

Finding out the facts about ourselves in relationship to alcohol, however, is but the first step we must take. If we do not accept these facts, then this is nothing more than an interesting but useless exercise. Acceptance of the truth about ourselves with regard to alcohol is absolutely essential. We dare not sugarcoat this truth, minimize it, explain it away, distort it, or deny it altogether. We must own the facts that come out of our drinking inventories. After all, this inventory is by ourselves, about ourselves, and for ourselves. It tells us about the lives we have lived, not as others see our lives, but as we see them.

Owning this information rather than simply gathering it is of utmost importance here. In effect, we must *internalize* this newly discovered knowledge about ourselves. We must take it in, make it an integral part of our thoughts about us and who we are. We must admit, acknowledge, and accept our alcohol problems for what they are.

Having found out the facts about the connection between our drinking and our problems, and having prepared ourselves by accepting these connections, we are ready for the most important action of our lives. With regard to our ability to control our drinking consistently, we must surrender to the obvious: *we do not have consistent control over either our behavior while drinking or the drinking itself.*

In effect, alcohol has already defeated us. The battle is over, and for many of us, it will have been over for quite some time. It is only our stubborn refusal to accept defeat that keeps us compulsively challenging our clearly more powerful foe.

But while we may have lost the battle with alcohol, the outcome of the war is still very much an open issue. By surrendering to the facts about our alcoholism and accepting our powerlessness over alcohol, we will have opened the door to eventual freedom from our obsession and the compulsion to drink. Despite all the complexities of our individual – and even perhaps unique – cases, one thing is abundantly clear: *it is alcohol itself that feeds our obsession with the stuff and our compulsion to drink it regardless of the consequences.* If we do not drink, we cannot get drunk. And if we do not get drunk for a sufficient period of time, this awesome obsession will leave us. We will finally come to know freedom.

Getting free is one thing. However, *staying* free is a more complex business, one that involves a great deal more than stopping the flow of alcohol into our bodies. Sobriety is not only about freedom from the compulsion to drink alcohol. Sobriety is also about the quality of our lives as nondrinking people, our goals, purposes, satisfactions, and ultimate concerns. We will study this more thoroughly soon.

For the moment, however, our point has been made. If we are to recover from this disease, first we must surrender. It is our fantasies that will keep us ill. The truth will set us free.

CHAPTER 12

In Search of Self

Some people seem to know a great deal about themselves. They can give an accurate account of who they are and what their values, attitudes, and motivations are. Most of the time, they are good at predicting their reactions to situations and have a good idea of what feelings may be coursing through their bodies at any point in time. We say about these people that they are in touch with themselves.

To other people, the self is like a mysterious island wrapped in mist and partially hidden by dark waters. For these persons, self-identity is a question mark, and their personal values, attitudes, and motivations are largely unknown to them. They are often wrong about their feelings and usually are uncertain as to how they might react to various situations. These people are said to be out of touch with themselves.

In a sense, people have either very good or very poor *self-intelligence*. Just as we have IQs or intelligence quotients, we also have SIQs or *self-intelligence quotients*. Taking both types of intelligence into account, we can see readily that a person might have a soaring IQ but fail spectacularly on an SIQ test. With a very high IQ, he could solve differential equations with half of his brain and analyze a complicated Bach fugue with the other half. However, with a very low SIQ, chances are good that he couldn't tell you whether he was angry or sad at any moment in time, why he married the person he did, or what his true motivation might have been for entering his field of study. A person with a high IQ and a low SIQ can tell you who Beethoven and Stravinsky were, but doesn't know who *he* is.

As a rule, we alcoholics need to raise our SIQs. Most of us should slow down when we stop drinking and examine who we are, what we feel and believe, and how we are likely to react to situations. In our interactions, we need to see our own behavior clearly and to be able to judge its impact on others realistically.

When we stop and think about it, it is not at all surprising that we learned so little about ourselves during our drinking years. Alcohol doesn't generally lead to a high SIQ. Because it is a depressant chemical, it is more likely to lead to numbness of feelings and denial of self than to a rich inner life of feelings and a constant awareness of self. When intoxicated we were not very perceptive of the needs of others or of ourselves. In withdrawal and the various states of illness we call hangovers, we were usually feeling too sick to feel much of anything else. On those days, we worried more about meeting the demands of our jobs or families and just getting through than we did about earnest self-analysis.

Is it any wonder that we don't know who we really are when we sober up? Drinking alcoholically isn't likely to give anybody a stable sense of identity. When sober, we think, act, and feel one way. When drunk, we think, act, and feel another way. Often, our intoxicated beliefs, feelings, and actions are at odds with our fundamental core values about ourselves. After a particularly bad night of drinking or acting out when drunk, we are stunned and shamed by actions we would never have committed sober. Guilt and remorse are the companions of many of us as we thread our way through alcholic lives that we cannot understand. *Alcohol smashes up our sense of identity*. A great conflict between our intoxicated beliefs, feelings, and actions and our sober beliefs, feelings, and actions lands us in a painful quandary: *we end up not knowing who we are*.

The search for ourselves is not easy nor is it painless. We may not like what we uncover, and the implications of what we find out may make us very afraid. The search for self, however, can be exciting too, and real knowledge of who we are can lead us to peace, serenity, and freedom. But how shall we begin to find out who we are?

In the AA program, members are urged to make a searching and fearless moral inventory of themselves. This suggested approach to self-knowledge is an important step forward for many recovering alcoholics in coming to grips with their strengths and limitations.

Timing, however, is an important issue to which recovering alcoholics should pay attention. Knowledge of self need not happen all at once. In fact, it can't. Moreover, life as it unfolds will present us with multiple opportunities to examine ourselves. We must not fall into the trap of thinking that a single intense self-appraisal is all that we will need. AA recognizes that more than a single personal inventory is necessary; its steps also include provision for a continued personal inventory over time.

There is another timing issue in our search for self-understanding. Knowledge of self simply cannot be rushed. If we push ahead too fast, we may end up doing more harm than good to ourselves. The act of peeling away the layers of self is not painless. Much of what we will uncover will not be pleasant. Some of it will cause frank anxiety, guilt, and depression. We need to recognize this from the outset and to take steps to insure that we will avoid flooding ourselves with more emotion than we can possibly bear. Getting in touch with our feelings is a good thing, but being devastated by them is not.

Self-analysis is definitely an art that requires patience, practice, and instruction. We alcoholics often are not particularly big on any of these characteristics. Impatient, impulsive, and resistant to teaching from others, we tend to rush right in and do things in an extreme way. If a little bit of something is good, then a whole lot of it has to be better. It is interesting to note that this same unbalanced attitude characterized our relationship to alcohol where more was usually seen as better.

In the search for self-understanding, however, the issue is not really one of more or less. The question of *when* things get revealed is the important one, and the matter of *how* we are to go about arriving at these deep insights is also critical.

As a rule, a thorough self-analysis should not be considered until the person has established a solid base of abstinence from alcohol. As our sobriety deepens, we will be able to take increasingly more penetrating looks at ourselves. For some of us, these deeper views of self will not become possible until we have maintained abstinence from alcohol for as much as two to five years. This does not mean, however, that persons must wait two to five years to start looking at themselves in recovery. Some self-examination must begin rather immediately, and to delay this necessary activity is just as dangerous as plunging ahead foolishly. It is the question of *degree* of activity that is at issue here—not all or nothing. Alcoholics will have to do at least some looking at self early in recovery. How much of this will be feasible or desirable early on is often too individual a matter to make general recommendations. However, there are some things that can be done.

In the beginning of our recoveries, most of our search for understanding who we are should center on our alcoholic drinking, its origins, consequences, and implications. At this stage of recovery, identification and understanding of ourselves as alcoholics is the crucial activity, and we must not allow ourselves to be distracted from pursuit of this particular body of knowledge. How did we drink? When did we drink? What happened when we drank? What were we like as drinking alcoholics? What will we need to do in order to stay sober? How did alcohol affect our bodies, our minds, our families? These are the critical questions we need to ask about ourselves during the early months of sobriety. During this period, we will probably find it necessary to look at certain very upsetting and guilt-provoking things we did while drinking. There is no other way to deal with such shameful things but to admit them openly and honestly to ourselves first, and then to get them off our chests by sharing them privately with some trusted other person.

As our sobriety deepens, our priorities should begin to change. Whereas alcohol-related matters were the big issues in our early months and years of sobriety, later we should begin in earnest to tackle fundamental questions of who we are, what we value and believe, what we want from life, and how we are to proceed toward self-fulfillment and satisfaction as sober people.

The defenses we had learned and used in our active alcoholic periods must now be overcome if progress is to be made. While we may no longer be denying our drinking, rationalizing or minimizing it, or blaming it on others, our lives may still be influenced heavily by these over-learned coping mechanisms. In our roles as parents, for example, we may try to deny problems with our children, rationalize such problems away, minimize them, or blame them on other kids, the neighborhood, or our children's teachers. These drinking-related tactics are not appropriate to a sober life and they will have to give way to accurate, sensitive, and realistic perceptions of ourselves and others.

Defenses, however, are almost automatic. We have used alcoholic defenses to such a great extent to conceal and justify our drinking that they will come into play quickly and naturally in our everyday lives as sober persons. As a result, without intense work on ourselves many of us will continue to be literally blind to our actions and their impact on ourselves and on other people in our lives.

Many times we alcoholics see our *intentions* in our interactions with others but we don't see our *actual behavior*. We may think something like the following: "I am acting with the best of intentions in this situation. Therefore, my actions must be having a good effect on these other people." Or we may say something like, "I know it is not a good thing to have a big ego and act in a grandiose manner. Since I know this and I don't intend to act that way, I couldn't possibly be faulted in my dealings with others." Sometimes we alcoholics can be caught banging our fists on the table in a rage while announcing to anybody fool enough to listen that we have given up getting angry because it isn't good for our sobriety!

The many discrepancies that can occur between our words and our actions don't mean that we are hypocrites or liars bent on deceiving ourselves or others. Most often such discrepancies mean little more than that we are ill-trained in observing our own behavior realistically and accurately. It is ironic that people continue to ask the very difficult and complex question of *why* do they do what they do, when they really are largely unaware of *what* they are doing in the first place. We alcoholics are often really not very good observers of our own actions. Of course there are exceptions to this rule, but the effects of alcohol on us as well as the defense we have learned in coping with our alcoholism do not favor accurate perceptions of ourselves. Most of us will have to learn how to see ourselves clearly and realistically in sobriety. This won't happen quickly or easily.

There are other reasons why it is hard to see our own actions clearly. Many of us have difficulty in being attentive to the here and now of human interaction. It is often our own thinking that distracts us. Focusing on the future and various worries and plans, we fail to see what is going on right before us. Or we obsessively think about difficult situations and people with whom we are involved and give most of our energies to these things rather than to the persons we are with. In effect, we often seem to have trouble staying in the "here and now"; we get too preoccupied with the "there and then."

At times we have trouble seeing our own actions because we are too caught up with what others may think of us. This makes us anxious and fearful of rejection, neither of which helps us to get relaxed, accurate glimpses of ourselves.

Whatever the reasons, if we hope to come to know ourselves better, we will have to develop the habit of trying to look at ourselves objectively. It is a good practice to check ourselves out at various times of the day as we go in and out of situations and interactions. These personal "check-outs" or "snapshots" may include questions like the following: "What am I feeling right now?"; "What am I doing in this situation?"; "How am I reacting to this person?"; "What is my body telling me about myself right now?"; "If my neck could talk, what would it say to me? My clenched fists? Tight jaw? Sour stomach?" All of these questions are directed toward the larger issue: *what* are my typical actions and reactions? Once we really do understand what we are doing, we may or may not choose to search for the reasons why. Sometimes we are able to change unwanted aspects of ourselves simply by paying attention to them. Often we will never know the precise reasons why we do certain things. Fortunately, knowledge of the *whys* of our actions is not always necessary for changing them.

What sort of things must we find out about ourselves if we are to stay sober and be comfortable while doing so?

First, we need to pay close attention to our *attitudes*. Here we need to be concerned with three things: attitudes toward life in general, toward ourselves, and toward others. How do we look at life? Do we tend to play up the negative in the world and ignore the positive? Are we thoroughgoing pessimists? Do we expect the worst and then go out and look for it? Are we constantly complaining about life and the raw deals it has handed us?

It is often the case that these negative, cynical, and pessimistic attitudes are a holdover from our drinking days when our lives were indeed nothing to cheer about. In sobriety, however, these attitudes regarding life must give way to some optimism and enthusiasm. It isn't necessary to become a Pollyanna in order to stay sober. In fact, unrealistic optimism can be as dangerous as pessimism, since the fantasy of impossible expectations must eventually yield to the cold bath of reality. For alcoholics, dashed expectations can lead quickly to a drink and a drunk.

Instead of either pessimism or Pollyanna, alcoholics need hope. *Hope is made up of a reasonable desire mixed with a reasonable expectation that this desire can be met.*

In addition to looking at our attitudes toward life in general, we need to review our attitudes toward ourselves. Most of us do not emerge from years of alcoholism with our self-esteem intact. Typically, our drinking and its negative results led to very poor self-regard, which took the form of either an "inferiority complex" or a grandiose posture that tried to hide the low self-esteem. Our best antidote to this alcoholism-induced dumping on ourselves is acceptance of the disease basis of our illness. *We alcoholics were not bad people trying to be good people, we were ill people trying to get well.* If we could have done better in life during our drinking years, we would have. Given this awesome, mind-shattering disease called alcoholism, most of us probably did the best we could.

In effect, alcoholics are not to blame for having developed alcoholism. No victim of a disease is blamed for developing the illness. But while we were not to blame for becoming ill, we are responsible for doing something about our illness. Acceptance of the disease concept of alcoholism does not excuse our present behavior or "let us off the hook." In actuality, understanding of our true condition forces upon us the obligation to care for ourselves—to take responsibility for our lives and our behavior.

Being responsible as a recovering alcoholic might begin with our first forgiving ourselves. Punishing ourselves for our illness is not a responsible act, nor is it right for us to criticize ourselves harshly. For many alcoholics, peace and contentment in sobriety will not come until we can look in the mirror and genuinely like and be willing to care for the person we see there.

Perhaps the second greatest benefit of becoming able to forgive and accept ourselves is that this helps us to forgive and accept others.

How do we habitually approach other people? Are we resentful and envious? Do we rush to gossip, judge, ridicule, and condemn? Are we too critical of others, too demanding of perfection in them, too controlling, dominating, or intolerant? It is important for us to think about these questions, for being at ease with others while seeing them realistically is a marvelous achievement, one that will reward us many times over. When we alcoholics are at peace with our fellow human beings, we are at our best. In sobriety, we do not thrive on bitter conflict.

A second major set of issues concerns our ways of going about getting what we want. At the most basic level, this may be a matter of honesty versus dishonesty. Lying, cheating, or stealing to get what we want is not likely to give us the inner security and freedom from fear we will need to stay sober. As a rule, alcoholics do not function well with a guilty conscience. Our private lives cannot become too disconnected from our public ones if we are to stay comfortable with ourselves.

Honesty versus dishonesty is but one important issue in how we go about getting what we want. There are more. Manipulation of others versus influence of them is another thing we need to look at. There are many ways in which we try to manipulate. Provoking guilt is one commonly used tactic. "Look at all I've done for you and see how you are treating me now" is a guilt-ridden ploy familiar to most of us. So is "Considering how much you have hurt me, why don't you do this for me?" While we can often see how others try to manipulate us with these guilt-provoking tactics, we are usually unaware of using them ourselves.

Some people try to get what they want by becoming excessively dependent on others. This is a dangerous way of getting what we want: it not only sets us up for extreme manipulation by others, but it also puts us on the road to ultimate rejection. No matter how much other persons may be flattered or made secure by our dependency initially, in time they will come to resent it. Very few people are happy for long with "clinging vines" or companions who cannot care for their own needs.

Bullying others through threats, intimidation, and even active physical violence is not for sober people. Nor can we get by for long through other forms of "emotional blackmail." People don't like aggressive bullies and, for the most part, won't tolerate them for long, just as they won't tolerate complainers, whiners, and crybabies.

Sometimes we may be tempted to feign illness to get what we want. Not only can we get a day off from work, we often get the undeserved sympathy of our friends. In time, however, our friends will tire of our endless complaints about our headaches, stomach pains, mysterious heart ailments, and so forth, that drive us to our beds when we should be taking care of business. Getting ill all the time is really not the way to go about getting what we want out of life.

Withholding love, sex, or friendship is still another way some people try to manipulate others to do what they want. These particular methods usually boomerang on us and are likely to produce frustration, anger, and resentment rather than positive outcomes.

There are a lot of ways of trying to get what we want from other people and from life. However, most of these ways are not workable for alcoholics trying to stay sober: the road does get narrower as we try to live a socially useful, ethical, and personally fulfilling life. For the most part, there are still only a handful of virtues here—honesty, integrity, hard work, creativity, and sensitivity to the needs of others.

Our search for ourselves must also include our *feelings*. As recovering alcoholics, we need to be able to identify and acknowledge what we are feeling in any given situation. This does not mean that we must always reveal these feelings to those about us. Being aware of our feelings is one thing while acting them out is quite another. There are many situations in which nobody—including ourselves—will benefit from unbridled emotions. In general, however, the importance of staying in touch with our feelings cannot be emphasized too strongly. An alcoholic walking about with a great deal of unrecognized anger or rage is like a gasoline can looking for a match.

Some of the feelings we need to recognize and, if possible, do something about are: depression; self-pity; anger, hostility, and resentments toward others; fear, anxiety, and panic; loneliness, isolation, and alienation; frustration, despair, and hopelessness. It should be obvious that some of these things may be beyond self-analysis and may require professional help.

Finally, our *beliefs, knowledge,* and *skills* form an important part of finding out who we are. As recovering people, we need accurate understanding of ourselves, our disease, and the worlds in which we live. Our beliefs and knowledge about these things are important because they give us the bases for our actions. Learning what we can do well and what we can't will give us some appreciation of our strengths and our limitations. Not everybody is born to be an Igor Stravinsky or a Babe Ruth. For the recovering alcoholic who can't carry a tune or bat a ball, music and baseball are not reasonable career choices, and no amount of wishing will make it otherwise. The same alcoholic, however, might make a superb pilot, a fantastic chef, or a great television news commentator.

In the final analysis, self-knowledge is the light on the path to continued sobriety. Knowledge alone may not keep us sober, but without it the paths into our futures grow darker, not brighter.

CHAPTER 13

Alcoholics Anonymous: Myths and Realities

Despite its presence on the alcoholism scene for fifty years, Alcoholics Anonymous is often a misunderstood organization. Myths about AA have persisted in spite of the fact that accurate information about this important program is widely available. For those of us who are thinking about AA involvement, an accurate and sensitive picture is very much needed. Alcoholics Anonymous has saved countless lives, changed the course of many more, and brought the light of hope into more homes in America than any other single approach to recovery from alcoholism.

Perhaps its extraordinary success in helping alcoholics constitutes one of the reasons why AA is both much loved and much misrepresented. For the alcoholic who is still compelled to continue his destructive drinking, AA gets distorted for obvious reasons. After all, if a person isn't serious about recovery, it is easy to make a few AA meetings and then tear the program down. Spouses and employers who may be unfamiliar with Alcoholics Anonymous are easily misled by the alcoholic's protests that he "has tried AA, and it isn't for him because" they make him do this or that, or because it is this type of program or that type of program. Some—but certainly not all—health care professionals may show hostility to AA simply because they erroneously perceive it to be in competition with them for patients and tighter health-care dollars. In actuality, professionals of all kinds—physicians, psychiatrists, nurses, psychologists, and social workers—are greatly needed by recovering alcoholics, and cooperation is in order—not mistakenly perceived competition. While AA's traditions do not permit it to be associated with any outside profession, institution, organization, or religion, members are more than willing to cooperate with knowledgeable, well-trained, and sensitive professionals from all health disciplines.

Perhaps the first myth that needs to be dispelled is that AA forces people to admit publicly to being alcoholics. *AA has only one requirement for membership: a desire to stop drinking.* It does not force its members to do anything. Even its Twelve Steps to recovery are suggested, not required. Members can call themselves anything they choose. Most will decide eventually to refer to themselves as alcoholics, but some will not. There are people in the program who refer to themselves simply as "members of AA" and not as alcoholics, problem-drinkers, or any other alcohol-related term.

A closely related myth is that AA forces people to stand up in front of others and tell all the horrible things they did while drinking. *Public confession of one's deeds while drinking is not a requirement of membership in Alcoholics Anonymous.* Once again, there are recovering alcoholics who choose to tell their life stories in and outside of AA, but this is not a requirement. Actually, many AA members quickly tire of hearing endless rambling accounts of drinking histories. Many members refer to these histories disapprovingly as nothing more than "drunkalogues." What most members prize are accounts of how other people are living sober today and how they go about achieving peace, happiness, and fulfillment without alcohol.

Opinion to the contrary, *AA is not a prohibitionistic organization.* AA does not condemn the social use of alcoholic beverages by all persons. The Fellowship emphasizes abstention for its members because alcoholics have proven time and time again that they cannot consistently manage either their drinking or their behavior while drinking. While abstention from alcoholic beverages is a critical first step for the newcomer to the Fellowship, AA's program of growth does not stop with the end of drinking. AA members distinguish between being merely "dry" and being "sober." To be dry and dry alone is not a very satisfactory condition. For the alcoholic, it is misery. At best, dryness is a "bridge" to the more complex state of *sobriety*. Whereas dryness refers only to drinking alcohol, sobriety refers to major changes in the recovering person's approach to physical health, emotional well-being, mental clarity, social relations, family life, work, love, and spirituality. Only the first step of AA's Twelve Step program of recovery deals with alcohol: "We admitted we were powerless over alcohol—that our lives had become unmanageable." The remaining eleven steps deal with learning how to live comfortably (and with fulfillment) with oneself and with others.

Alcoholics Anonymous is sometimes criticized because certain of its detractors believe it endorses a simple and naive disease concept of alcoholism. This misconception is difficult to understand since *AA, from its very beginning, embraced a subtle and complex concept of the disease*. By attending to the physical, mental, emotional, and spiritual aspects of alcoholism, AA anticipated very recent developments in modern medicine, psychiatry, and psychology—not only for the disease of alcoholism but for many other diseases as well. In 1935 AA was already embracing a psychosomatic view in which body (allergy to alcohol) and mind (obsession with alcohol) were joined to explain the origins and maintenance of the disease.

One particular biological concept, allergy, was advanced by a physician with great interest in and admiration for AA—Dr. William Silkworth. In the foreword to the 1939 first edition of the book *Alcoholics Anonymous* an invited statement from Silkworth entitled "The Doctor's Opinion" set forth the physician's beliefs that alcoholism was an allergic disorder. Silkworth wrote:

> We believe, and so suggested a few years ago, that the action of alcohol on these chronic alcoholics is a manifestation of an allergy; that the phenomenon of craving is limited to this class and never occurs in the average temperate drinker. These allergic types can never safely use alcohol in any form at all; and once having formed the habit and found they cannot break it, once having lost their self-confidence, their reliance upon things human, their problems pile up on them and become astonishingly difficult to solve.

Silkworth, of course, has not been shown to have been correct in his beliefs about alcoholism and allergy. In historical perspective, however, it is quite clear how he could have been led to this position. The notion of alcoholism as an allergy had been available since 1896, and given the then-extant body of scientific information, allergy was probably as attractive an hypothesis as any other. In any case, the founders of AA and early members, in keeping with what appeared to be respectable medical opinion of the time, concluded that alcoholism was an allergy of the body coupled with a mental obsession to drink alcohol.

Today, a variety of positions can be identified among AA members with regard to the allergy concept. There are those members who accept the hypothesis as fact and consider alcoholism an allergy to alcohol in part. Others make metaphorical use of the concept and think of it as a useful analog. Still others reject the hypothesis entirely and consider some other biological concept more plausible—or reject biological etiological factors entirely. And of course other members simply do not have an opinion either way.

Because of the central role of spiritual development in AA, many people confuse the Fellowship with organized religions. *AA is not a religious organization, but is a spiritually centered organization.* The Fellowship is not an organized religion since it does not require members to accept a single concept of a deity, has no religious ritual, and enforces no single body of religious beliefs.

Although AA is a spiritually-based program, it is not allied with, nor wishes to be confused with, any sect, denomination, organization, or institution, and it clearly states this position in its traditions. Members of AA are not required to accept, practice, or promote any religious belief or concept. Members are encouraged to find a "power greater than self," but this external power can be construed in any manner that each person wishes. The AA group itself can serve as a power greater than self. For others, abstract concepts such as love or truth may serve as higher powers around which a life can be oriented and through which direction can be sought. For still other AA members, a higher power may be construed in terms of historical or legendary figures (Christ, Buddha, God, Yahweh, and so forth).

The AA emphasis upon spirituality in the form of a power greater than self serves the important psychological function of encouraging the member to seek out alternative bases for belief, attitude, and behavior. Turning one's will and one's life over to a power greater than self encourages the member to reexamine his or her own way of doing things and to seek out and practice alternative beliefs and behavioral patterns. Many members come to realize something like the following: "I insisted upon doing things my way, and it got me nowhere but deeper into trouble. It's time I tried it some way other than my own." In effect, such a statement is the beginning of AA spirituality and constitutes acceptance of the third step of the program: "We made a decision to turn our will and our lives over to the care of God as we understood Him."

The steps to recovery do suggest that belief in a higher power, as each member understands that concept, is of great value in the restoration of sanity and in finding a life of personal satisfaction and fulfillment without alcohol. But it is important to note that the AA higher-power concept is an entirely open and free concept. The member may believe what he or she chooses to believe, and nobody in AA can tell them to believe otherwise.

AA's emphasis upon the disease concept has led some to believe that the social movement ignores psychological factors entirely. In actuality, *psychological factors are given considerable importance in the AA program of recovery.* Moreover, a careful reading of AA literature suggests that these psychological factors carry some etiological weight as well. Step four is very much a "psychological step." In step four, members are invited to engage in a "searching and fearless moral inventory of ourselves." For most members, this step involves an extensive examination of past behaviors. It calls for a fairly classic psychological activity—intense self-examination with the purpose of developing awareness of self-destructive and self-defeating patterns of behavior. Depending upon the thoroughness of the inventory, the step can include an extensive examination of values, beliefs, feelings, attitudes, and motives as well.

That psychological factors are involved in the AA etiological view is evident from the following passages in the book, *Twelve Steps and Twelve Traditions*:

> Alcoholics especially should be able to see that instinct run wild in themselves is the underlying cause of their destructive drinking. We have drunk to drown feelings of fear, frustration, and depression. We have drunk to escape the guilt of passions, and then have drunk again to make more passions possible. We have drunk for vainglory—that we might the more enjoy foolish dreams of pomp and power.

The role of depression is remarked upon in the following passage from the same book:

> If temperamentally we are on the depressive side, we are apt to be swamped with guilt and self-loathing. We wallow in this messy bog, often getting a misshapen and painful pleasure out of it. As we morbidly pursue this melancholy activity, we may sink to such a point of despair that nothing but oblivion looks possible as a solution. Here, of course, we have lost all perspective, and therefore all genuine humility. For this is pride in reverse. This is not a moral inventory at all; it is the very process by which the depressive has so often been led to the bottle and extinction.

In AA, members recognize the importance of psychological matters such as resentments, self-pity, egotism, unrealistically high expectations, frustration, stress, sexual and love relationships, self-esteem, fear, anxiety, guilt, grandiosity, self-will, melancholy, depression, security needs, envy, power over others, control and domination of others, and fear of financial failure. For an organization that supposedly does not feel that psychological factors are important, the list is long indeed! Not only does AA involve itself with psychological matters, its activities are clearly and intelligently planned psychological processes. The AA group meeting, for example, could be a textbook example of the social-psychological processes that characterize healthy, strong, and positive human relationships: open, honest, and trusting communication; caring, respect, and consideration for others; commitment to the growth and well-being of self and others; and empathy for and identification with others. Many of AA's other processes and steps either implicitly or explicitly recognize the importance of both individual and interpersonal psychological processes in the recovery from alcoholism.

Critics of AA frequently confuse AA priorities with recovery goals. The ideal recovery in AA is not "dryness" alone, but a complex set of outcomes involving major changes in behavior, attitude, belief, emotions, and general psychosocial functioning. The first priority of AA is the achievement of abstention from alcohol, but abstention alone is not considered sufficient. The familiar AA slogan, "First things first," is in fact a simple reminder of the order in which things must be carried out. In the beginning, the newcomer to AA is urged to deal with his drinking first, to the exclusion of other problems that might involve family, financial, or employment matters. This concentration upon the drinking problem to the exclusion of other problems early on in recovery stems from the conviction that nothing else will get better if the drinking continues. As abstention proceeds, the member becomes capable of seeking solutions to additional problems. Alcoholics Anonymous is not only a program that concerns drinking; it is commonly referred to by members as a "program for living" as well. Of the twelve steps to recovery that form the heart of the program, only the first step ("We admitted we were powerless over alcohol – that our lives had become unmanageable") deals explicitly with alcohol, or – for that matter – even mentions alcohol. The remaining eleven steps of the program comprise a program for dealing with the broader issues and problems that confront all human beings, alcoholic or not.

In AA, members distinguish between being *dry* and being *sober*. To be dry and dry alone is perceived by members as a transitional state on the way to sobriety at best, and, at worst, a miserable, uncomfortable, and undesirable condition. "Dry but not sober" is a commonly heard description in AA that refers to a person who is not drinking but who has failed to come to grips with important aspects of self that involve values, attitudes, feelings, typical patterns of behavior, and personality factors.

Among AA members, sobriety refers to a complex, subtle, and multi-dimensional state in which aspects of the drinking personality, lifestyle, and worldview are no longer evident. Sobriety is, in effect, a change of consciousness, an altered state or, if you will, a heightened spiritual awareness in which elements of serenity, acceptance, contentment, gratitude, and joyfulness are evident. Words like "balance," "wholeness," "fulfillment," and "spiritual transformation" are necessary if the AA concept of sobriety is to be grasped and distinguished from mere dryness or abstention alone.

A further quote from *Twelve Steps and Twelve Traditions* illustrates the AA link between psychological factors and the road to sobriety:

By now the newcomer has probably arrived at the following conclusions: That his character defects, representing instincts gone astray, have been the primary cause of his drinking and his failure at life; that unless he is now willing to work hard at the elimination of the worst of these defects, both sobriety and peace of mind will still elude him; that all the faulty foundation of his life will have to be torn out and built anew on bedrock.

The belief that AA is hostile to psychological and psychiatric knowledge is unfortunate. Some AA members may have received inadequate treatment in the hands of poorly trained and inadequately educated professionals in the past. However, this unhappy situation is changing rapidly as the curricula of professional and graduate schools reflect the realities of the disease of alcoholism and more and more professionals are achieving accurate and sensitive understanding. AA, despite strong opinion to the contrary, is psychologically a very sophisticated Fellowship. Many of its concepts and procedures are psychology in action at its very best.

Finally, it is sometimes believed by certain people that AA's position on the necessity for abstention if alcoholics are to recover from alcoholism is purely an ideological position with no empirical basis. Moreover, these persons believe that modern science has proved AA wrong on this point and that alcoholics can be taught normal, controlled, or nonproblem drinking. Of all myths and misconceptions, this one is potentially the most dangerous because sufferers from the disease of alcoholism will place themselves at risk for grave and even tragic consequences if they embrace this myth.

The AA belief in abstention for alcoholics did not just appear out of the blue in a burst of ideological inspiration. It grew out of empirical observation in the real world. It grew out of direct observation of suffering too painful to bear, of tragedy and shattered dreams, of broken bodies, alcohol-related diseases, ended careers, and destroyed families. AA recognized early that a relationship existed between the continued ingestion of alcohol by alcoholics and the eventual but inevitable negative consequences of an active alcoholic life. In effect, AA's beliefs have come from literally hundreds of thousands of direct observations of men and women in the real worlds of small towns, cities, the suburbs, ghettos, and megalopolises. AA members have had plenty of direct experience with drinking alcoholics and with sober alcoholics. They don't report seeing much controlled or nonproblem drinking at all. What they do report is that life for countless alcoholics and their families improves beyond imagination when they get the message, stop drinking, and begin to work a Twelve Step program of recovery.

The scientific evidence against abstention, when viewed objectively, is unimpressive. The number of documented cases is simply too small for any responsible and ethical professional to announce to the world that a cure for alcoholism has been achieved.

These many myths and misconceptions about Alcoholics Anonymous should not stand in the way of any alcoholic seeking help with this devastating disease. Nor should one or two unsatisfying experiences. Meetings differ greatly in type, format, size, time, and membership. Alcoholics seeking to understand AA should go to a number of these different meetings in order that the range of meetings can be experienced directly. There are speaker meetings in which one or several main speakers talk about their experiences drinking and sober. In these meetings, speakers focus on what it used to be like when drinking, what happened, and what it is like now that the drinking has stopped.

In contrast to speaker meetings, discussion meetings permit all members to share their experience, strength, and hope with each other. Discussion meetings are usually *closed* meetings in the sense that only alcoholics can attend, while nonalcoholics are urged to attend *open* meetings. Speaker meetings are usually open to everybody—alcoholics and nonalcoholics—although some speaker meetings are closed.

Step meetings concentrate on the twelve suggested steps of the program to recovery. Usually, members take turns reading the step out loud, including supporting text, and then discuss how they have worked the step or used it in their lives.

There are quite a few special meetings. Women's groups, men's groups, gay groups, and other special-need groups are available in some communities. Recovering alcoholics who attend a special-group meeting usually attend other groups as well. Most members are encouraged to find themselves a home group to establish a stable base for their programs.

For the spouses of alcoholics, older children, parents, lovers, and other concerned persons, the Al-Anon program provides much comfort, guidance, and support. Al-Anon holds its own meetings, and operates in a manner very similar to AA. Anybody whose life is attached to an alcoholic in a significant way should explore the Al-Anon program. Also, Alateen is available to the teenage children of alcoholics. In general, alcoholic families in which all members get involved in AA, Al-Anon, and Alateen are families that are maximizing their chances for a contented and satisfying sobriety for all members.

There is far more to AA than we can cover here. The interested reader is urged to consult AA literature directly. Sources of this literature are given at the close of the book, as are the complete Steps and Traditions of the program.

Alcoholics Anonymous is truly a great and wonderful program for alcoholics. Without question, it has been the most effective recovery program available to alcoholics for over half a century. All alcoholics owe it to themselves to give this important program a serious and fair trial.

CHAPTER 14

More on Powerlessness

As we have seen, we alcoholics are people who cannot *guarantee* our drinking or our behavior once our drinking starts. This imperfect control over alcohol is characteristic of many of us from the very beginnings of our drinking lives. Many of us got drunk the first time we drank. Others of us had to drink for a period before problems showed up. But in time, as our disease progressed, these early problems with control for all of us gradually shaded into extreme vulnerability to alcohol: we began to lose all choice over when we would drink, how much we would drink, and how we acted when we drank.

Filled with remorse, frightened, ashamed, and shaking inwardly after a particularly bad night of drinking, we promised ourselves and others that this had gone far enough, that we would never drink like that again. Our promises, however, were short-lived and we ended up once again remorseful, frightened, ashamed, and ill. While we refused to admit it to ourselves or to others, we had become powerless over alcohol.

But if we were to recover, our refusal to recognize our inability to exercise consistent control over alcohol had to give way to surrender to the facts. We had to see and acknowledge that we were powerless. And as we have seen, modern science has now shown that the reasons for this powerlessness over alcohol are to be sought in the chemistries of our brains.

These thoughts on powerlessness are interesting enough, but what does it all mean? Does powerlessness mean that we alcoholics are helpless, that we cannot take any actions at all that will improve our lot? Does it mean that we are doomed to lives of futility, failure, hopelessness, and inevitable tragedy? Does powerlessness over alcohol imply the kind of helplessness that psychologists have shown to lead to massive depressions? The answer to each of these questions is a definite *no*. Powerlessness over alcohol, properly understood and acted upon, is the stepping stone to health and eventual happiness for alcoholics, not to further illness and despair.

Other things being equal, no human being can remain satisfied for very long in a state of complete powerlessness. We alcoholics are no exception. Since our own personal bases of power are no longer of any use to us as far as alcohol is concerned, we must turn to help from a source *outside* of ourselves.

Alcoholics Anonymous has for years recognized the importance of a power greater than self to which alcoholics may turn for aid, comfort, and guidance. The AA concept of a higher power is a spiritual concept and not a religious one. In the Fellowship of AA, this means that each member is free to find a power of his own choosing. For many recovering alcoholics who have maintained their faiths in organized religions, finding a suitable higher power is not a problem. Faithful Catholics, Baptists, Lutherans, Methodists, Jews, and so forth, may turn to the teaching of their churches and the God of Christianity or Judaism for guidance. Agnostic alcoholics, however, who wish not to endorse a personal God-concept from some organized religion may have a more difficult search for a power greater than self.

In Alcoholics Anonymous, new members are often urged to use the AA group itself as a power outside of self to turn to for guidance and support with their alcoholism. For some persons, this is a solution that will suffice until the entire issue of spirituality can be wrestled with more profoundly. The typical AA group possesses an impressive body of collective wisdom about alcoholism and alcoholics. Anybody seeking an answer about an alcoholism-related issue is not likely to be given wrong information or suggestions from an AA group. A newcomer to AA may not like what he hears at a meeting or may not understand it, but the talk about alcoholism and what to do about it is usually right on the money.

Using the AA group as a power outside of self early in recovery is attractive for several reasons. For the alcoholic struggling with the possibly difficult issues posed by spirituality, the group as a higher power is concrete, tangible, and immediate. There is nothing mystical or supernatural about an AA group, and the act of placing one's trust in such a group has a simplicity and reality that neatly avoids the abstractions of complex spiritual questions. Moreover, by agreeing to accept guidance from a group of recovering alcoholics, a newcomer to AA is showing a willingness to listen to other views of alcoholism. And since his own way of looking at his alcohol problem has not been helpful, opening his mind to other perspectives is certainly in order. Early in recovery, the alcoholic needs to listen to others who have succeeded where he has failed.

While the AA group can serve as an entry point to a spiritual way of life, many recovering alcoholics will find it necessary to move beyond this temporary device to deeper understanding. But what can one believe if one wishes not to embrace conventional religious concepts? Are our choices restricted to agnosticism versus organized religion? Perhaps not.

Regardless of how we define God to ourselves, one thing is clear. God is our *ultimate concern* in life. Paul Tillich, the highly regarded theologian, told us this over twenty years ago. From Tillich's perspective, human beings are rarely without a god, since each of us shows, in some manner or another, an ultimate concern in life. Some people make money a god. They pursue riches, wealth, and financial advantage with passions worthy of zealots. They dream of possessions and acquire them only to dream of still other possessions. They live, eat, drink, and breathe money. Life for these people is essentially a series of deals. In effect, they have turned their will and their lives over to money.

Sex can be another ultimate concern or higher power. Men and women throughout history have wrecked their own lives and created pain and chaos in the lives of others by their sexual obsessions. Of course, compulsive sexuality may reflect the operation of still other ultimate concerns. The male who must seduce every female he meets rarely respects and loves women. The motivations for this behavior are more likely to be variants of hostility, contempt, and the obsession to dominate. In a more general sense, the need to dominate and control others regardless of sex is an indication of obsession with power itself. Power as such is not necessarily a bad thing. Used properly and in the service of others, power may contribute to the common good. In the hands of power neurotics or those who must compulsively pursue power over others as an end in and of itself, power as an ultimate concern usually leads to destructive results.

These three ultimate concerns—obsessive concern with money, sex, and power—constitute the higher powers of many people in modern societies. It should be abundantly clear by now that these higher powers do not reliably lead to peace, satisfaction, fulfillment, or purposeful and meaningful lives. More often, they lead to conflict with others, disappointment, unfulfilled longings, disillusionment and despair. We alcoholics must understand the risks we take in pursuing these particular gods to the point of destructive obsession. To recover from alcoholism, we must cultivate inner peace and serenity through lives of balanced emotions and motivations. The turmoil generated in the intense, compulsive struggles over money, power, and sexuality is not for us. Inner turmoil, regardless of source, is an important trigger that gets us thinking about drinking as a way to resolve our inner discomforts and outer conflicts with others. And, of course, once the drinking starts, the body chemistry will sooner or later insure its continuation beyond safe levels.

Alcoholics especially should be able to see that many higher powers abound in our everyday worlds. Having made alcohol and, in some cases, other drugs into ultimate concerns, alcoholics are familiar with at least one destructive higher power. When an alcoholic is driving home late at night from a bar or an office party, it doesn't take much imagination for us to see that he has turned his will and life over to a depressant chemical, *alcohol!* Sadly, however, many drinking alcoholics will refuse to admit this obvious fact and will continue to make alcohol their ultimate concern while rejecting any possibility of a more positive and beneficial higher power for themselves. For these persons, alcohol, drinking, and intoxication are somehow defended as reasonable, rational, and real. A more constructive higher power, however, is often dismissed as mere "superstition," "mysticism," and "irrational."

Sex, power, money, alcohol, and drugs are but a few of the ultimate concerns or higher powers that people obsessively pursue. Gambling at cards, on horses, or in other ways is a form of behavior that can reach the addictive level and constitute a potentially destructive higher power. Fame and prestige can also drive some people to wretched excess, while others will become obsessed with food and fashion. For some of us, obsession with another person will become a destructive ultimate concern. When we find ourselves completely dependent upon another person for our happiness, self-worth, security, and identity, we have made this person our god. This is, of course, a dangerous position to be in since we have given the other person control of our emotions, behavior, attitudes, and even our minds. Moreover, another person upon whom we have become completely dependent may walk out on us, divorce us, take up with somebody else, become terribly ill or die. What then, if we have turned this other person into our higher power?

In actuality, then, the world of higher powers contains many more choices than we may have realized. It is not simply a matter of religious belief versus atheism, nor of a personal god versus doubt. One may, of course, choose to look at one's own search for a higher power in these terms, and for a particular alcoholic these may be perfectly acceptable paths to spiritual awakening. But approaching higher powers as ultimate concerns can broaden creative exploration.

Although we may not have considered it in this context, *love* is an ultimate concern or higher power through which we may find meaning, purpose, strength, and guidance in our lives. As some people assert, *God is love!* And indeed, we could do much for ourselves and others if we were to take seriously this notion of God as love. But how would this work?

When we place our faith and trust in love as a higher power, we are accepting love of self and others as a tangible and powerful force. (Love of this nature should not be confused with romantic love nor with the love that we may find among certain close-knit families.) The love that is referred to here is an objective and all-encompassing state. It is not restricted to one's lover or one's family. This love is a more universal guiding force for our thoughts, actions, and behaviors with regard to living things generally. It is a reverence for life.

Love is a demanding and often difficult higher power, since many of the actions that we personally might wish to take are, in reality, harmful to ourselves or to others. It is not loving to ourselves to continue to drink alcohol if we are alcoholics. Nor is it loving to our children, spouses, or friends. Driving a car drunk cannot be thought of as loving to anybody including ourselves. Drinking at work expresses contempt for ourselves, our coworkers, jobs, and employers. Ending up drunk at a family reunion is not the way to show our families and our relatives that we care about them. For us alcoholics, the message should be apparent with regard to alcohol: *love is about sobriety and not continued drinking*.

Can love as a guiding force help us in other ways in life? Can this ultimate concern give us comfort and support on our jobs, in family relationships, in our neighborhoods, and in business affairs? Can it be an anchoring principle around which we may order our lives?

Acting out of love may not bring us money, fame, and power over others. But centering our lives on love of self and others will provide us with a basis for our actions. Love can guide us in all of our dealings in the world and give us more than enough comfort and support. The trick, of course, is that we must be willing to give it a try, and we must also be alert to its impact on ourselves and on others. If we can set aside our cynicism and place our trust in the power of love in human relationships, we are likely to find rather amazing results.

Turning our will and lives over to the care of a force like love does not mean that we must give up all say in our everyday affairs and defer constantly to the wishes of others. Loving ourselves is an important priority since we cannot love others if we despise ourselves. And it is not loving ourselves to put ourselves in an inferior position in our dealings with others. Nor can we truly love others if we passively accept all of their ideas, attitudes, and actions, including the most destructive ones. Love requires us to be firm, caring, and assertive with our children or friends who seem poised on the verge of actions that are not in the best interests of themselves or others. Sometimes love requires us to take risks with our friends. In telling them the truth about their actions, we may be risking the friendship. In effect, love is a tough higher power to serve. It is not all roses and lollipops or peaches and cream.

For those of us who have suffered from the disease of alcoholism, we must like and respect ourselves if we are to remain free of alcohol. And if we are to sustain our recoveries, this positive self-regard is not a luxury, but a necessity. It is when we despise ourselves for our real behavior in the world, when we engage in negative appraisals of our motives, ethics, and actions vis-a-vis other human beings, that we begin to consider alcohol as a way out of our discomfort. We may not always like the way things go, but with love in our hearts for ourselves and for those with whom we must get on, we will continue to like and respect ourselves. And above all else, we will be sober.

As we have seen, then, admitting to powerlessness over alcohol does not mean we are helpless or hopeless. There are actions we can take and other powers to which we may turn for support, guidance, and meaning. If we place our faith in love, we will have hope. These three things – faith, love, and hope – are the raw materials from which a comfortable sobriety is built.

Appendix

The Stories

The following stories are based upon interviews with recovering alcoholics. While I have changed names and locations in order to protect the identities of the persons involved, the rest of the details are exactly as told to me. No attempt has been made to change these accounts in any significant way. The stories are to the best of my knowledge and ability as close to the informant's accounts as I could possibly get them.

As these stories show, alcoholics are like snowflakes. Each is absolutely unique. Yet, when we look again, they are all very much alike. There are many faces of alcoholism. And as these personal accounts reveal, there are many miraculous stories as well.

Julia's Story: Death and Resurrection

Whenever I hear or read that alcoholics are supposed to be irresponsible, undependable, and unreliable, I don't know whether to laugh or cry. As an alcoholic woman, I wasn't any of those things. Alcohol helped me to be just the opposite—super-responsible and determined to meet the demands and expectations of others. If anything, alcohol took away my *self*. As a drinking alcoholic woman, I came to live for others, not for Julia. In a very real sense, I died meeting the obligations of others. And alcohol helped me to do that. But I'm getting ahead of myself.

My early life was spent as the child of an alcoholic father and a mother who was addicted to pills. My father was far from down and out . . . quite the contrary. He was a highly placed executive in a major corporation. We lived in elite neighborhoods and wealthier suburbs. Because of my father's very high income, we wanted for nothing. But while my younger sister and I had material abundance, our early emotional and spiritual lives were empty. There wasn't much love in our home.

I remember that my father's routine never varied. Every night of the week, he took the train back from the city, drove home from the station, walked into the house, and went straight to the bar. He'd pour out eight ounces of gin, throw it down, and then read his paper. Before dinner, he'd drink another eight ounces of gin. With sixteen ounces of gin in him before dinner, it was not unusual for my father to sit down at the table in a blackout. This was some early life. With the drinking by my father and the pills for my mother, there was a lot of parental and maternal deprivation. I remember reaching out for my mother and I remember her turning away. I was left vulnerable.

In my family, I was the scapegoat for a lot of problems. I was the "troublemaker," the "bad kid," the one who would fight with the other kids in the neighborhood. My younger sister was the "bright one." She was articulate, smart, capable, and on the ball as far as my parents were concerned.

After a while, in my parents' eyes, I became the "one who can't make it." The one who "falls apart." I was "pretty but stupid."

At sixteen, I found a soul mate. His name was Paul and he was the child of two alcoholics. Paul's father had walked out some years before; he lived with his alcoholic mother near us. Paul's mother was a very successful female executive. She was the Chief Executive Officer of a major corporation, but that didn't stop her from getting drunk. Paul and I would go over to his house and find the C.E.O. mother lying drunk and passed out on the living room floor.

We were two rich kids with all the money we wanted and all the things that money could buy. But we didn't have affection, intimacy, and love in our homes. So we nurtured each other. Like two lost waifs in the night we traveled together and clung to each other, giving the support, love, and care our parents could not give.

Along with meeting Paul at sixteen, I also had my first drink. I drank eight ounces of vodka at a party (just like my father!) and passed out. I was sick and had to be taken home. After that, I didn't drink until I was twenty-one. Aside from not wanting to get sick, I didn't want to get fat. I was on my way to being a professional model, prom queen, and a debutante. After all, my mother said that the only way I was going to make it was to be charming and beautiful so I could marry a rich guy. In college I didn't drink. I was becoming a nice upper-middle-class eligible young lady. For me, it wouldn't be socially acceptable to think of a job and a career. Marriage was the goal. A good marriage. Life in the affluent suburbs of America with a hardworking and, of course, rich husband.

I met Peter at a deb party. He was a West Pointer, a man with his heart set on a distinguished and highly successful military career. We agreed not to get serious. A year later we were engaged. I got married to run. I was in love, but I also wanted somebody to take care of me.

My second drink came with my father-in-law. I'll never forget how Peter's father came striding into the home in his officer's cape and hat. He was career army too. In his hands he held a bottle of booze and he said, "Well, Julie, if you're going to be in the army, then you'll have to learn to drink like a lady."

Well, I'll tell you, this time I loved the feeling. This time I didn't get sick – I got loaded. I found out that alcohol did something very special – it killed my feelings. I could perform beautifully. My in-laws were no problem, marriage was no problem, the world was no problem. With the magic elixir alcohol in me, I felt nothing. No feelings of fear, anger, sorrow, anxiety, or anything. Alcohol, by letting me feel nothing, made me feel good.

Peter and I went off to our first assignment just as the war in Vietnam was heating up. We were in the States and the war over there seemed remote. At first it seemed too distant to touch us. But then, people we knew – other young officers – began to leave for Southeast Asia. We became aware of our first stirrings of concern.

In the early 1960s, I had my first child, and I went into an immediate postpartum depression. The doctors did not know how to deal with it. They gave me Valium, something I definitely did not need. I took the Valium, and when it didn't help the severe depression, I medicated myself with alcohol. It was eight months of hell. No sleep, no eating. The black night of the soul. My mother was a severely depressed woman and so was her mother before her. I guess it runs in the family.

Near the end of my depression, a popular magazine arrived at our house. There on the cover was a photo of one of our best friends from West Point. He was no longer the lively, handsome young officer we knew. There on the cover of the magazine was his lifeless body, his guts bursting out of a shocking rip in his lower abdomen. Peter and I were stunned by the horror of this sudden intrusion into our home of this far-off war. Shortly thereafter, our friends began to come home in body bags. Death was suddenly very real and all around us.

Three weeks after this first shock, my husband was ordered to Vietnam. This was the last time I allowed myself to have rage. When he came home and told me he was going to Vietnam, I screamed at him. I suppose it was then that I began killing myself with alcohol. That's when I lost hope. When I gave up and died.

Peter went to Vietnam and I went home to my parents' neighborhood where I had grown up and where it was definitely not posh to go to war. Nobody there would discuss the war. Fortunately for me, there was a nice, warm, fatherly psychiatrist who lived near me. Although he did give me tranquilizers and did not detect my depressive illness, he did tell me I was heading for alcoholism and should stop drinking. But he was warm and loving. Other than my friend Paul with whom I had grown up, this psychiatrist was the only person besides my husband who would listen to me and give me love and understanding.

A year after my husband went to Vietnam, I had a day that I will never forget as long as I live. I was sitting in my home in my old neighborhood listening to the radio when I heard that my husband's battalion had come under heavy attack. They had been overrun and the men were missing. I was frantic. I rushed to my parents' home. My father chose that moment to get dead drunk. My mother had overdosed on pills. In the midst of my panic, I somehow got the police to the house and got my mother to the hospital where her stomach was pumped.

I came home, poured myself some drinks, and waited for the dreadful news from the Mekong River Delta. My husband was one of only five United States advisors to come out alive. He watched almost all of his men get shot down and killed. One of his best friends died in his arms.

Peter came home then from Vietnam and we returned to service life. For me it was a return to the kind of drinking that allowed me to carry on, to be a good soldier's wife, to do my duty. Drinking like a lady and an officer's wife was to drink to blot out the anger, terror, horror, and rage. We sat with other officers and their wives in the security of the clubs and listened to the boasting, the tales of bravery, combat, killing, and medals won. And we all drank. Perhaps for the same reasons: the men to kill the pain of killing other people, the women to kill the pain of powerlessness.

At this time, death came to sit at our table. It was all around us as more and more of our friends were going back to Vietnam for further tours of duty and returning home in body bags. Peter, as a result of his new assignment, would often accompany the remains of old friends back to their hometowns, to the sorrows of their wives, sweethearts, parents, brothers and sisters, and old friends. It was a terrible time, but it got worse. I gave birth to my second child, and once again I went into a deep and profound postpartum depression. I knew Peter would probably be returning to Vietnam as were his friends, and this didn't help things at all. My depression was very bad. This time, however, it was finally treated correctly. Instead of tranquilizers, they gave me antidepressants. It was incredible how quickly my depression lifted. The tranquilizers and sedatives had given me insomnia and hallucinations. On antidepressants, however, I returned quickly to normal. I got to feeling so good, I forgot to use birth control pills. Once again, I found myself pregnant. This would be my third child.

The day I found out I was pregnant, I could hardly wait for Peter to come home. He walked in the door and I rushed to tell him the good news. Before I could get the words out, he said, "I'm going back to Vietnam." I felt small, hopeless, and dead inside.

Peter went back to Vietnam and I went to live near his parents. I was carrying the baby and going out of control. They once again gave me the very thing I did not need—tranquilizers! I became hysterical, crazy, hallucinating, and depressed. I had the baby and became even more depressed.

Peter came home from Vietnam. Disillusioned with what he saw as the administration's betrayal of its own armed forces, he resigned his commission. The war had left its mark on him. He decided to enter the seminary and to devote his life to God and service to others. By 1970, we were all together on friendly soil: Peter, me, and the three children. My drinking, however, was now totally out of control. I was drinking around the clock. I suffered from bouts of depression and insomnia. I functioned, but inside I was a dead lady. For four years, I did all that a wife and mother was supposed to do. I cooked, cleaned, shopped, washed clothes, and watched my children. But I drank to maintain. Except for the fact that I moved around and met the demands and expectations of others, I had died. For all intents and purposes, I was a dead woman. No feelings, no sorrows, no pain. And alcohol made all of this possible.

In 1974, I was literally brought back to life by two other sufferers from the disease of alcoholism. Both were members of Alcoholics Anonymous. One of these people, a student at the seminary my husband attended, took me to my first meetings. He was sober only two months when he held out his hand to me and took me to AA. My husband knew that I was carrying bottles in my purse, hiding alcohol in salad dressing bottles, and even in the washing machine. He had called this fellow seminarian for help out of concern for me.

The other person who helped me became my sponsor. In her drinking days many years before, she had been a prostitute and a favorite of certain mobsters. She herself came into AA through a mob leader who brought her to meetings in a bulletproof car!

My sponsor loved me. She showed me compassion. This former prostitute and gun moll showed me what it was like to suffer and what a human being was supposed to be about. She told me, "Julia, you're a scared and lost bird. I'm going to have to help bring life to you. First, we're going to get you a bikini for some sensuality around here, and then we'll get you back to school." She told me I had a fine mind and that I had better start using it or it would get me into trouble.

I did all those things. I bought a bikini and learned to like lying on sunny beaches, I went back to school and finished a master's degree. I stuck to AA and made my sobriety the core of my life.

Today, I'm a happily married, sober, productive woman with a daughter in college, two at home, and a husband in the pulpit. The death of the past is over. Life is precious now, and very real. Feelings flow through me as naturally as does water through a river bed. I can feel, think, see, touch, and be touched by others. I am alive now, and often joyously so.

In the recovery from alcoholism there are these amazing, strange twists and turns that come our way. This upper-middle-class deb had died, and it took an alcoholic clergyperson and an ex-prostitute to give me back the most precious gift of all — the gift of life.

Brian:
The Kid Everybody Thought Was Bad

I was a real symptom of a sick family. In a way, you could say I was the kind of symptom people write books about. Both of my parents were alcoholics, my older brother may be one, and one of my sisters is a recovering alcoholic like me. My family was torn apart by alcoholism.

My dad was a manager, an engineer. My mother had a college degree and taught school. But that didn't keep either of them from drinking themselves to death. Although their death certificates probably state otherwise, both of my parents died of alcoholism.

Except for my parents' drinking, our home was a typical middle-class household. My dad went to work and my mother, after teaching school for a time, stayed home to raise the kids. We weren't rich but we didn't want for anything.

By fourth grade though, I was compulsively stealing. There was no reason for this. I stole things from the other people in the family. They got so that they were frightened to leave anything around.

From grades four through seven, my school work took a nose dive. As my parents' drinking increased, my grades went down. Trouble for me came as my parents slid deeper into alcoholism.

I had my first drink at twelve. It was some bottles of beer that me and the other kids found in the woods. We drank it warm. It filled me up. I didn't like the taste.

I started skipping school a lot by seventh grade. My marks fell down to where I was doing F work in everything. But instead of failing me, my teachers gave me Ds and bumped me along. I guess they didn't want me in their classroom for another year. About this time, I became aware that there was something very odd about me, something very strange and different. I began to believe that I didn't have a conscience because I could steal and lie and it had no effect on me at all. When I got confronted about my stealing, I'd try to lie my way out of it first. If that didn't work, I'd throw a temper tantrum. I'd have these fits of rage in which I'd strike out at objects around me. I wouldn't hit people but I'd smash a wall in the house.

School was a real pain to me. My older brother was a straight-A student. He was smart and a good student. But everybody compared me to him. All my family went to the same schools. My father was brilliant and he had gone to the same school. My mother had been class valedictorian. I was constantly being compared to my parents, brother, and sisters. It was tough to have to face up to that.

The teachers bumped me along until I got into high school. I first got drunk in eighth grade when I was fourteen years old. I drank a half quart of vodka. The vodka was stolen by a friend of mine from his girlfriend's house. I got drunk, but he didn't. Because I got so sick, I didn't drink for six months. But then, in the winter of the school year, I began drinking regularly on Fridays.

I hung out with boys fourteen to seventeen years of age. We either stole the liquor from our homes or got somebody to buy it for us. We'd drink it in the woods so we wouldn't get caught.

At about fifteen, other drugs came into play. I started taking speed. Some of the guys I ran around with started breaking into drug stores. They would get pills of all kinds.

There were older guys who came into our neighborhood to deal heroin. They were young men from the city in their early twenties. And there were some guys from the neighborhood who were eighteen- or nineteen-years-old who were into heroin. They showed me how to do it. I started injecting from the very beginning. My first time on heroin, I loved it. I was fifteen and the euphoria that came with injecting heroin was out of this world.

Alcohol, however, was my mainstay. I didn't have real good connections to heroin, and, anyway, it was too expensive. A bag of heroin those days cost ten to twenty dollars. And you could get a couple of quarts of wine for only two bucks. I drank wine.

I quit school at age sixteen. My parents were furious with me. I didn't care. Emotionally I felt no warmth from my family. I was disconnected from them. I was very cold and distant with them. I got to where I wouldn't show up at home for two to three days at a time.

By then, my mother's drinking increased to where she wouldn't leave the house. She lay on the couch in the living room and drank. My father brought a couple of bottles home for her every evening after work. He'd drink. She'd drink. My two sisters became the mothers. They would cook, clean, and shop.

I began to spend a lot less time at home. And I began getting into more and more trouble with the law. Petty stuff. Fighting with some other kids, assault when drunk, public drunkenness, disturbing the peace, breaking the tops off parking meters.

I stole a lot of cars at this time. I didn't sell them. I drove them home when I needed a ride. We'd come out of a bar at 2:00 a.m. and need a ride. So I'd steal a car, and when I got home, I'd leave it at the top of the hill near my house. It got like a junkyard up there with all the stolen cars.

By the time I was eighteen, I was using heroin pretty regularly. Alcohol was there too but heroin was getting to be the problem. I'd go on runs—inject heroin for two, three, six months and then clean up. I was addicted by eighteen years of age.

At age eighteen, I was no longer living at home for six to eight months of the year. I'd go out and then bounce back in for awhile. I was living a real transient life. One morning when I was at home, my mother died of alcoholism. She weighed seventy pounds and was just forty-seven years of age. I think she died of the DTs—acute withdrawal. Our doctor said it was a series of strokes that killed her, but I knew it was alcoholism.

My reaction surprised me. I felt needed by the family and I felt close to them. Later, I grieved a lot with a girlfriend over my mother's death. She was kind to me but broke off with me over the drugs. She wouldn't put up with my heroin use.

I supported my habit by dealing drugs. I sold pot to finance my narcotics. Other people around me had gotten into armed robbery and serious breaking into drug stores. I stayed more with pot dealing.

At one point, we had a warehouse. I was keeper of the place—kept it open six days a week around the clock, watched the money, and counted the drugs. I was twenty-two years old and I had no family contact at all. About this time, I got a dirty needle and a bad case of hepatitis. A friend who used the same works as I did got it and went to the hospital where he died. A priest got me to go into an alcohol detox at about that time.

This began a long series of hospitalizations and legal problems. I ran from one part of the country to another. West Coast to East Coast and back again. I crisscrossed the country several times in the early 1970s. I began bouncing in and out of detox centers. Drugs of all kinds were now in the picture—alcohol, heroin, marijuana, hashish, mescaline, and so forth. The arrests for various crimes began accumulating—breaking and entering houses, drug possessions with intent to sell. I shoplifted cigarettes, power tools, and appliances, and sold them to support my habit. And I took up with a lady who did some hooking and dealing. We both got arrested.

I never got involved with violent crimes. I stayed away from the stickups of dealers, masked and armed robberies of pharmacies, and that kind of stuff. Sooner or later the guys who went in for this hard-crime act went to jail, and I didn't like the thought of jail.

I began to have stretches where the heroin use would just stop. Then it would be heavy alcohol use and I'd end up in an alcohol detox sick and shaking. In five years, I had 150 hospitalizations for alcohol and drug detoxification. Sometimes I'd have as many as three a day. I'd go out, get drunk, and the police would bring me back.

Eventually, the alcohol detox places wouldn't take me back. They were sick and tired of me. I started to go to the state hospitals. At this time I was only twenty-five years old, and it felt like I had lived a least a half a century.

The last two years of my drinking were in the late 1970s. The heroin was out of the picture and it was mainly alcohol. There was no connection to my family now and no other long-term relationships. The girlfriends were all gone and so were the guys I drank with. I was down and out and on Skid Road. I was alone.

A judge sent me to a detox center because I had been caught with drugs on me and charged with possession with intent to sell. The judge knew me and my record. He wanted to lock me up. After detox he gave me a suspended sentence and ordered me to a long-term drug treatment program. I stayed four months until one day I got up and walked out the front door and never came back. I drank for forty-eight hours and almost literally destroyed myself.

Somehow I ended up in an alcohol detox and twenty-eight-day program where I started attending AA meetings. I had tremendous mood swings in early treatment. From despair to euphoria and then back to despair. A lot of disconnected feelings. Gradually, all of this cleared, and when I got out, I took the first real job of my life. At twenty-seven years old, I started selling shoes. I lived in a halfway house and after a year, me and three other alcoholic guys leased an apartment and shared the costs. We went to AA meetings together and it worked out fine.

About this time, I heard from my sister. My dad was in the hospital dying of cirrhosis of the liver. I went to see him. He was bitter and resentful toward me. I guess he died that way. When I saw him, he was hooked up to a maze of tubes and machines. It was pitiful. While he lay there dying of alcoholism, he told me that his doctor had told him that he could still have a couple of drinks and control his drinking. Of course no doctor had told him that. He made it up.

My dad died of alcoholism, but my sister and I have been given a daily reprieve from the horrors of the disease. At my father's hospital bed, I found out my sister had gone through her own hell with the disease and was recovering through AA.

The family really pulled together after my father's death. I was sober. My sister was sober. As amazing as it may sound, I was accepted back into the family. Today, there is real connectedness, warmth, and love for us. Our parents are gone but we are together now, strong and caring.

With the help of AA, I went back to school after being sober for eighteen months. I got my high school equivalency even though I thought I could never do it. I did a couple of years of college and made good marks.

My life today isn't always easy, but it's better in every way than the hell of my active alcoholism. I've had to work on myself through personal therapy for several years in addition to three AA meetings a week. But it's all working.

Before I found AA, I thought I was nothing but a bad seed that would turn out rotten. Today I know I was truly a symptom of a family disease. Alcoholism destroyed my parents and, in doing so, almost got me too. I am thankful that I survived to come to know the truth about myself. I have a conscience, I hold deep feelings for myself and those around me, and I have the capacity to love others. Today my life is about honesty and service to others. For these and many other reasons, I am grateful to the many people who helped me come to know and accept the truth about myself. It's a long pull up from Skid Road and drug addiction to where I am now. And I'm not about to forget that.

Steve: Last Rites at Twenty

Nobody in my family drank. As far as I know, my grandparents never drank and there was never alcohol in their home. My mother didn't drink and neither did my father. My older brother has been a social drinker for many years and doesn't have the problem at all.

My early years weren't unusual. We weren't wealthy, but we weren't poor either. As I remember them, things seemed okay up until about the age of ten. My father was quite a bit older than my mother and I really didn't get along with him. He seemed very demanding and set in his ways. I was close to my mother. When my father and I fought, my mother would take my side.

At the age of ten, I started hanging out at a friend's house. His mother was an alcoholic and there was alcohol in the house. My friend and I began to get into his mother's supply. There was plenty of alcohol at that house. It was always available.

Although I had a very high IQ and had done well in school, my drinking progressed rapidly to the point where by eleven years old I was getting drunk and either missing school or going drunk. The gym teacher found alcohol in my lockers and called my father. He punished me physically and my mother would intervene. I'd promise not to drink again, but of course the promise was broken and I drank.

Alcohol got me in a lot of trouble at school. I was rebellious. I took suggestions as orders and refused to do them. I skipped school a lot and ran away from home often. I was in and out of court for violating curfews and other minor things. They sent me to training school three times, the first time when I was twelve or thirteen. The last time they sent me, I ran away. When they caught me, the judge put me on restriction and suggested strongly that I consider joining the service. I was about sixteen years old at the time.

Looking back on this period, I can see that I was a full-blown alcoholic at fifteen. I was a blackout drinker from the beginning and there is much I don't remember. I thought I was a bad kid meant to get into trouble.

Eventually I did join the service. I was seventeen years old and had quit school after finishing the eleventh grade. I completed basic training, and on my first leave, I got drunk the first night. After that it was successive AWOLs and getting drunk. I ended up AWOL in Mexico drinking tequila. When I returned to base, I was told that if I didn't shape up and quit drinking, they would kick me out. I didn't want that to happen so I went underground with my drinking. I'd still get drunk, but I'd confine it to nights and I'd show up for duty in the mornings. At this time I started having seizures. I was about eighteen years old. Both a military doctor and a civilian doctor in my hometown told me I would have cirrhosis by the time I was twenty if I didn't stop drinking.

I didn't stop, but I kept my drinking hidden as much as possible. I was discharged honorably from the service and got about $3000 mustering-out pay. I started out for home on a bus. Three months later, after a maze of hotels, motels, and bars, I ended up home with only a couple of dollars in my pockets. I was in blackouts most of the time. Somehow or another, I stopped off in New York City for a month. There I woke up in all kinds of strange places with black eyes, bruises, and aches and pains of various kinds. I didn't know how I got them.

I returned to my hometown broke. But I could always find a job. I liked restaurant work and ended up a chef. This was a drinker's paradise. Now my disease really took a turn for the worse. I started having terrible seizures. It was five years of going in and out of hospitals.

By the time I was twenty, I had cirrhosis of the liver. My entire family was called to the hospital by the doctor who said I was not going to make it through the night. They gave me the last rites.

I fooled them. I lived. Because I lived, I said to myself, "Those doctors don't know what they're talking about. I didn't die, so what do they know!" I got out of the hospital ten days later and promptly started drinking again.

Within two weeks, I was back in the hospital. I had severe seizures, yellow jaundice from the liver disease, and blood was coming out of my mouth, nose and other body openings. After that it was a nightmare. Over the next few years, I was in virtually every ward of the hospital at least a dozen times. I knew the first names of all the doctors in the entire hospital! I guess I had about sixty serious hospitalizations in a five-year period. I still had cirrhosis of course, and I continued to drink on top of it. Why I didn't die, I truly don't know. I had the last rites five times in five years. The doctors would look at me in amazement and shake their heads. They truly did not believe that I continued to live.

After a time it got so I couldn't function. I had been working a month, two months, or six months, and then I'd go back in the hospital again. But I became completely unemployable.

You know, I had four friends when I was growing up. They were all alcoholics like me and we hung out together. All four died in their late twenties and early thirties. One died of cirrhosis, two were thrown through the windshields in alcoholic car crashes, and the fourth was murdered selling drugs in a big city. Five young men. Four dead—and I should have died. I went to all their funerals but I didn't see that alcohol and drugs had caused their deaths. Perhaps I couldn't see that or didn't want to see that.

By Christmas Eve of 1974 I was a very sick man. I had gone to a local park alone and started to drink. As I was later told, I became unconscious and was dying in the snow. Blood was running out of my body from everywhere. Some nuns found me there and called for an ambulance.

In the hospital I was connected to eight machines to keep me going. There were tubes of all kinds running in and out of my body. I have a rare blood type and I needed blood badly. Some local people from AA knew that I was in the hospital. They came and gave blood for me. All over the area, AA groups found out about me and prayed that I would recover. Looking back on this Christmas Eve, it was truly moving. All of these AA people who did not know me personally had given me blood and were pulling for me to recover.

The same doctors who had attended to me before gave me a two-percent chance of surviving, and if by some miracle I did survive, they said I would be a vegetable for life. To make matters worse, during a seizure, I pulled the tube out of my throat and blood gushed out of my mouth. The veins in my esophagus had ruptured again. My mother, who was at my bedside, screamed for help and once again my life was saved. I pulled through that night and the next day which was Christmas. Once again, the doctors were astonished.

For three months I remained in intensive care. My liver was so screwed up that I weighed over 360 pounds. I was literally nothing but fluid and fat. My color remained completely yellow and my legs were like tree trunks. But I was alive. One by one they disconnected the machines and took them away.

As soon as my temperature was down, my doctor told me I was going to the AA meeting that was held in the hospital. I didn't want to go but he insisted. He made me go, and I went to my first AA meeting in a wheelchair with two intravenous bottles still hooked up to me and strapped over the back of the chair. My legs were still like tree trunks, my stomach was swollen like a huge pumpkin, and I was yellow. The people at the AA meeting were startled. They thought that a mistake had been made and that somebody had brought a corpse into the meeting.

In my first meeting I was a divided person. One side of me sighed with relief and said, "At last you're home. Here at last are people who will understand you." The other side of me said, "I don't need this stuff! Let me out of here!"

In the beginning I was a real mess. I'd scream at people to get away from me. I don't know how AA people could stand me but they did. I blamed everybody and everything for what had happened to me, but I didn't blame the disease of alcoholism.

People put up with me, except for one woman. She was tough as nails and two years sober. When she got sick and tired of my nastiness she gave it right back to me. She said, "Cut it out. That's enough of that kind of talk. I'll take you and that wheelchair and kick you down the stairs!" I had finally met my match. She helped me by reading me the riot act. After that, I began to shut up at meetings and behave a little better.

I met my sponsor then. He came from a completely different life than I had. He was a former politician, millionaire, and clubman. He had lost a fortune, yachts, homes, and everything. He still had his wife and one year of sobriety on AA. I thought he was ten years sober but here he was, and he got me for his first "pigeon." Today he points to his head full of gray hair, which was black when I found him, and says, "See this, I got this over you!" We both laugh at that one.

After putting up with me, he told me one night, "Look, I can't work with you. Maybe I'm just hurting you and you had better find another sponsor here in AA to work with you." I was crushed. I felt I was losing everything. He said, "Maybe you'll be willing to try it somebody else's way for a while instead of your own." I was totally dumbfounded. Nobody had managed to get that thought through to me before. I settled down and even tried to listen at meetings.

One night my sponsor called and said he couldn't take me to the meeting and I would have to find a way to get there myself. I was furious! I said to myself, "I'll fix him, I'll get drunk."

Instead of drinking, I hitchhiked to the meeting and there he was, sitting down with a smile on his face. I started to tell him what I thought of his trick, but he cut me off right away. "Sit down," he ordered. "Take the cotton out of your ears and stick it in your mouth." I did what I was told to do. That was the turning point.

I stuck to AA. In fact, I made it my life. At eleven months of sobriety, I went back to the doctor who had attended me. He could not believe what had happened to my liver. He shook his head and stared in amazement. The liver had returned to normal size and position. I was truly a miracle.

For a number of years, I lived in a big house across the street from the hospital. When an alcoholic like me showed up and I had an empty bed, they sent him to me. Over four years, I took in seventy-four guys with severe alcohol problems. At any point in time, I had eight or nine guys in my house trying to get a toehold on sobriety.

At a year and a half of sobriety I got my high school diploma, applied to college, and was accepted on my second anniversary of sobriety. I finished a B.S. degree and then an M.S. I've stayed very active in AA. I've done everything there is to do in AA—group secretary and treasurer, general service representative, and central service delegate. I helped with the first young people's group in our town and that group really saved my life. In my first years in AA, I had many speaking commitments. Sometimes I'd talk twenty times a month to other AA groups.

My life today is rewarding. I am grateful to be an alcoholic, and as strange as it may sound to some people, grateful for the pain and suffering I had to go through. I had to experience that pain so that I could be the person I am now. Because of my past suffering, I can help the people who have the same disease as I do. For that, I am truly grateful.

Mary's Tale:
Alcoholism Really Is A Family Disease

There were fourteen kids in my family and my parents had to work hard to support us all. My dad was a laborer who had to quit school after grade five. My mother finished a high school education.

We were poor people. My mother cooked on a wood stove and we ate government surplus. Funny, I still get hungry for corn meal! But there wasn't much money for anything and I remember childhood as a tough time.

I was a loner. I'd sit upstairs in the chimney corner and read for hours at a time. We were the only Catholic kids in our hometown, and the nearest parochial school was sixteen miles away. Going to school that far from our hometown didn't help my feelings of being different. It was tough to make and keep friends.

When I turned sixteen, my family bought a car so I could drive us all to school. I also went to work at this time. In high school, I was putting in twenty to thirty hours a week at a local grocery store. Friday nights I'd work until closing at 10:30 p.m., and on Saturday I'd work from 5:30 in the morning until late at night. In the summer, I would put in sixty hours a week. When I look back on my childhood and teens, I can see now why it took me twenty years after college to learn how to play!

In the early 1960s, I went off to school on a full work scholarship. In exchange for thirty-five hours of work a week in the college food service, I got my tuition, room, board, and fifty dollars a semester. I was poor as a church mouse, but I was intelligent enough to get through without embarrassing myself. In fact, instead of doing the usual five years and two summers on a full work scholarship, I finished up in four years and four summers.

I can remember how exuberant my mother was when my acceptance letter to college arrived. Also, without money and clothes, I knew I'd feel out of place in a wealthy school. To cover up, I wore my work uniform to classes so the other kids wouldn't see that I really didn't have any clothes. None of this was particularly good for my self-esteem.

I can remember my first drink—a glass of green beer on St. Patrick's Day when I was a senior in college. It wasn't any big treat or thrill. I guess mainly I was afraid of drinking it. Getting past the housemother in the dorm was a real fear to me. She sniffed us all to make sure we didn't drink.

I really didn't drink in college. Actually I didn't start drinking until about six years after graduation from college.

My first job was as a programmer at a university. I got involved with systems work for about four years and ended up working on various academic administrative systems. During this period I got married. At this time I didn't drink regularly, and drinking really wasn't the reason why the marriage ended. I guess I got tired of being a caretaker. Anyway, the marriage didn't work out, and in 1974 I separated.

It was after my separation that I started drinking and enjoying drinking as I ventured out socially. Drinking, however, wasn't a problem at this time. It was something that I would do socially.

I met my second husband in 1976 and we dated for three years before getting married. While we got along fine during our dating years, marriage seemed to change it all. He became male dominance personified. I was always under his thumb and he began to cut me down constantly. He was suspicious to a fault and very insecure. Out in public he was kind and nice. At home, it was verbal abuse and shredding me. When I tried to talk about the marriage he clammed up and insisted that if we had problems they were mine, not his.

As the marriage went from bad to worse, I began drinking alone. He was working in a different state and I was left to amuse myself five days out of the week. I was starting to drink regularly after work, but it still wasn't a lot. I'd come home from work, put on my jogging clothes, and have a couple of drinks. Most of the time, I spent my evenings alone drinking and reading.

The marriage finally ended, as anybody would have predicted, and I moved to another state. I moved to be near a man I had met. This was a difficult time for me. I couldn't move into my own house for several months and my things were in storage. My boyfriend and I would start out drinking in the afternoons. It was scotch and the sports on TV, followed by a bottle of wine with dinner. I was getting concerned about my drinking, but when I moved into my own house it slowed down greatly.

But three months later, it was like a volcano erupted. Suddenly, I was deeply in trouble with alcohol. My boyfriend and I had some problems and I felt pushed aside, but that couldn't explain it. Here I was, the hard-working lady from a poor family who had literally pulled herself up by the bootstrings. There wasn't anything I couldn't do if I wanted to do it. But I couldn't stop drinking. Alcohol had defeated me—and in a relatively short time. Once I started to go downhill, I went fast. Fortunately, I had enough knowledge of alcoholism from my own family's experience to see what was happening to me. I stopped in time. I promptly went into a treatment center.

Of my fourteen brothers and sisters, eleven of us became alcoholics! My oldest brother has a master's degree in a scientific field, but he's been in prison and rehabilitation hospitals because of his drinking. My older sister is a highly placed executive, but she drinks tons of beer. I've seen her shake in withdrawal and not know what was going on. The two brothers just ahead of me are both alcoholic; one is recovering in Alcoholics Anonymous while the other is still drinking.

The brother immediately below me is sober five years on AA, but the next brother down is a severe active alcoholic. Of the three next younger sisters, two are not alcoholic, but the youngest is recovering through AA.

Of the last four kids in the family, one sister has gone through very bad bouts with alcohol, but the last girl in the family still drinks socially. My two youngest brothers both have terrible alcohol problems; one of them has already gone through rehabilitation treatment for alcohol and drugs.

Where did all this alcoholism come from in our family? My maternal grandfather was an alcoholic, and I've always believed my mother was really a potential alcoholic.

Fourteen kids in my family and eleven of us are alcoholics. Who says alcoholism isn't a family disease!

Charlie: Booze and Blues

Music and alcohol got all mixed up together in my life. By the time I turned fourteen, I was playing in bands in my hometown and looking forward to a life as a jazz musician. As a kid, my heroes were all the greats of modern jazz. I looked up to masters like John Coltrane, Ornette Coleman, Charlie Parker, Miles Davis, and Thelonius Monk. I wanted to be like these guys, play like they did, and live like they did.

Jazz musicians unfortunately have a large self-destructive streak—you could even call it a romance with self-destructive ways. When I was a kid, I quickly came to the conclusion that the way to be noticed by the older musicians was to be "far out." My fellow musicians liked the unique, the unusual, the odd. They didn't care at all about having a "straight" life with a square job, house in the suburbs, 2.3 kids, and a dog. Dedication was to the art of playing jazz and nothing else. We studied music long and hard. We went out and played jobs, and we drank and drugged as hard as we had studied. The attitude was definitely nonconforming. We were "cool" and "hip." To be sober and straight was to be "square."

Since I had come from a family with a history of problem drinkers, I guess I was set up for alcoholism by the added madness of the jazz musician's life. Three of my grandparents had alcohol problems. So did my father and several of my uncles and aunts. All of these people, however, were functioning alcoholics. They all achieved a great deal in life despite their disease. Among these alcoholic relatives there was a nurse, a manager of an industrial corporation, an editor of a major city newspaper, and a politician.

At fourteen, I was playing in a club called the "Bucket of Blood" in an Eastern industrial town. When the fighting got real bad, we'd strike up "The Star Spangled Banner" and everybody would come to attention and quiet down for a while. Sometimes, however, we grabbed the drums and horns and split out the kitchen door as fast as we could.

Booze, marijuana, and amphetamines were always around then. Personally I preferred the booze. Marijuana made me lose my sense of time and amphetamines wrecked my nervous system. A couple of shots and beers, though, and I felt fine. I quickly found out that after a couple more, I felt even finer.

I graduated from high school and went off to music school when I turned sixteen (I had been a bright kid in school, and at that time they would double-promote you—make you skip grades and move ahead). I ended up in college a couple of years ahead of myself. I could do the work, but I was socially still wet behind the ears. I lied about my age and told everybody I was nineteen. Sometimes, I'd tell people I was twenty-one. I don't know why, but I felt odd and different to be only sixteen when everybody was older than me.

As an undergraduate, I drank a lot, skipped classes I didn't like, and got straight As in everything I liked. My record looked like that of a split personality—all As and Ds. I played in bands on Saturday night and usually ended up partying until Sunday morning on the money I made. Sometimes the Saturday night drunks were disastrous, but usually I'd just get a good load on while playing a job and then come home. From the beginning, though, there was something definitely wrong about my drinking. From my first drink, I always wanted more. And when I got drunk, it was usually a bizarre happening. With alcohol in my system, I was the creative clown, always pulling off something nobody expected. I never fought or got violent. I didn't have to. I managed to get everything into a turmoil around me just by saying and doing the most outrageous things I could find to do. Drunk, I was Zorba the Greek or Scott Fitzgerald or an Irish poet . . . definitely a wild, Walter-Mitty streak in me that came right out when I drank alcohol.

After music school, I went into the service and played in a big service band and orchestra. This was four years of hard drinking, music, study, and acting crazy whenever I could get out of uniform and into town. I studied musical arranging, composition, and orchestration when I was in the service. When I wasn't drinking or playing, I worked incredibly hard at understanding how to write for all the instruments, writing many scores late into the night. During this time I wrote for concert band, symphony orchestra, jazz groups, and various chamber music ensembles. In a way I was setting up the pattern of my life—long grueling hours of hard work when sober, interrupted only by bouts of alcoholic drinking. Most of the time it was weekend drinking, but once I started to drink, I drank with a compulsion that was absolutely fierce. It was nothing for me to down five or six martinis, a bottle of wine with dinner, four or five brandies after dinner, and then scotch-and-waters too numerous to count, on into the night. When all the good stuff was gone, I'd switch to cheap cooking wine or anything else I could get my hands on. Maybe this is why I never became a daily drinker. I threw so much down in such a short time that I was just too sick in two days of drinking to go on.

I married after a couple of years and this slowed me down a little bit, but my pattern was now firmly established. On the one hand, I was a very hard worker and a super-responsible guy. On the other hand, I was a crazy, irresponsible drinker who did the unpredictable and drank with a thirst that seemed never to be satisfied. The hard-working, responsible part of me decided to leave music after the service, in order to go back to graduate school to get work that would suit a man with a wife and two babies. Through graduate school, I played music five nights a week to support my family and worked days as a research fellow. Long, brutal days and hard drinking nights. My marriage came apart at the seams when I started coming home at daybreak. I had met somebody else, and I thought I wanted out of the marriage even though it caused me, my kids, and the woman I was married to very great pain and suffering. I broke it all up — or rather alcohol helped me to break it up. I wasn't proud about any of this.

During this period when I was getting divorced, I was a mess. I felt like I wasn't in control of myself, that I was carrying out some crazy plan that I wanted but didn't want. I suffered horrible attacks of guilt and anxiety, particularly at night alone in the cheap apartment I had taken. I dealt with it all by getting drunk.

Despite all of this trouble in my life and despite my bouts with alcoholism, I got the highest grades in my graduate class and I received both of my advanced degrees with the highest possible honors. I went off to teach at a major university with a fresh doctorate and a bad case of alcoholism. I had remarried after my divorce, and this marriage was a typical alcoholic three-ring circus. When I was up, she was down. When I was down, she was up. We couldn't communicate. She hated my drinking with a passion. When I drank she usually went crazy. One Christmas Eve, she went so crazy she grabbed two bottles of rum and threw them through the picture window! I suppose my drinking had really started to bother her.

Finally my wife told me that she had had it with me. It was pretty much get sober or else. I did the "get sober" part of that command because I loved her and didn't want to lose her. I went to AA, and after a time I got to love it. In the beginning, I kept my advanced degrees to myself and tried to get the program at a simple level. Looking back on it, this was rather amazing. My life had been spent playing and writing complicated modern music, and my academic career was in a complicated science. But once I got to AA, a small voice inside me kept saying, "Just let it happen. Don't argue. Don't debate. You've done enough of that and look where it got you." I listened, watched, and kept it very simple.

In time, I found I had a higher power. My higher power isn't a conventional one, but that's okay since I'm hardly a conventional guy.

After several years in AA, my marriage really went on the rocks. This time it wasn't my drinking. (Ironically, the woman who had ordered me to AA had developed a problem of her own.) My wife went back to school for an advanced degree. Unfortunately, the times were not happy ones on the university campuses. There was much bitterness, anger, rebellion, and dope.

My wife got heavily into drugs, and from there it was an easy step or two into a long-delayed rebellion of her own. After a time of terrible suffering, the marriage cracked, as indeed most do when one alcoholic is sober and the other is drugging.

The way my marriage came apart was very painful. Moreover, I believe I hurt more in sobriety than I ever did drinking. In sobriety, I pretty much lost everything material—wife, house, cars, furniture, money, savings, and so forth. I felt every emotion there is to feel and then some. And I felt them for nearly five years after it came apart. But I didn't drink, and gradually my pain and sorrow ended. In time, I put my life back together again. I married again. This time I was sober.

Today, I am grateful for a lot of reasons. Sobriety has given me a way of life I never dreamed would be possible. I have a happy marriage, an interesting and challenging job, and friends I care about deeply. My life today is about knowledge tempered with wisdom and justice softened with love. It is creative and productive—more creative and productive by far than when I was actively alcoholic.

Chuck: The Chairman of the Board

I grew up in an alcoholic family. My father was a full-blown alcoholic. He raised hell in the family and made our lives miserable. The effect of his drinking on me was to turn me off to alcohol. As a teenager growing up and as a young man I swore I would never drink or smoke. And I didn't—at least not until I was in my second year of college. I did it to be part of the gang.

I went out with a group of fellows and we bought a gallon of red wine. We drove around and drank. I don't know why they drank, but I drank to get drunk. Funny . . . after all my promises to myself not to drink, not to be like my father, I drank to get drunk the very first time I picked up a drink.

I was sick for three days after this first drunk. To this day, I can't stand the smell of wine.

I didn't drink for a long time after this first drunk. I realized at some level or another that my drinking wasn't the same as the other guys. For one thing, I got hostile and they didn't. I tried to get into a fight with a cop who stopped us. While the cop wanted to throw me in the clink, the other guys talked him out of it.

I married in 1938, and two years later graduated from college. At this time my drinking was sporadic. But about four years after I got out of college we started having parties at home. Everytime we had a party, I'd get drunk. I was a friendly, sleepy drunk at this time and not violent. We had five kids in this marriage. Alcohol broke it up.

During the war years, I worked two jobs. From 8 to 5 I was a manager in a company making heat pumps, and from 11 to 7, I worked in a shipyard on the night shift. This is how I learned business. After two or three years, I quit the shipyard and concentrated on the manufacturing job. I began regular drinking.

On my job, I saw many things that needed improving. I had good ideas but they treated me like a kid and wouldn't listen to me. I got impatient, quit and started my own company at the age of twenty-nine. I rented space and started producing tankless hot water heaters. I sold all the heaters, found sources of new materials and the money to pay for them. I don't know how I managed to do all this since I didn't know beans about it. But the business was a success.

I was "controlled drinking" much of the time. One day out of five I'd be too sick to work, and then it became two days out of five.

In my late thirties, I developed pancreatitis. I already had a bleeding ulcer. All of this was caused by alcohol. The doctors wanted me to stop but I laughed and kept on drinking. A friend of mine, a chief of surgery, told me to quit or else. But he sat on his yacht drinking dark glasses of bourbon and he later died of alcoholism.

In time, I began to have violent attacks of pancreatitis. My pulse rate would shoot up and the pain was horrible. They put me on pills for the pancreatitis and I ended up stuck on booze and pain pills. After that I got hooked on sleeping pills. They were beautiful. I'd not only get a buzz on but I'd fall asleep during the day. I got to feeling so good, I fell down the hatch of my sailboat. They put me in a psychiatric hospital for three months where nobody mentioned alcohol or alcoholism! In fact, I had married again and my second wife would drive up to visit me in the hospital. They would let me leave the grounds for lunch with my wife and I'd have a few gins and beers. I'd go home weekends and drink there. Therapy was telling the psychiatrist everything he wanted to hear, and then it was wallet-making and wood-working. They gave me an IQ test and told me I had a very high IQ but that there was something wrong with me. I didn't reveal and they didn't confront. I was in this hospital twice. Each time I'd go home and get drunk.

I finally met a few people in AA. They took me to an AA-oriented place. I wouldn't stay very long—maybe ten days at the most. But I got introduced to AA. The lady who ran the place was strong on AA and there were several meetings a week.

I met my sponsor at this time, Fred S. He was a true AA guy. He would come to my house. When I got stinko, he drove me to a treatment facility out of state. I'd stay five days, come out, be all right for three weeks and then get into trouble with drink again. Fred stuck by me. He'd take me to AA and he didn't give up on me.

I had numerous hospitalizations. Most of these were for the medical complications of alcoholism: pancreatitis and other illnesses. I was getting desperate with myself. My most memorable emotion was fear. My wife was giving up on me. My doctor told me that if I drank, I'd die. I was out of control and couldn't stop. I was hallucinating.

I asked an old-timer in AA what I needed to do. He said you need to stop doing it your way and to try somebody else's way. A lot of people helped me. My brother was a big factor in my recovery. He came to see me in the hospitals and looked after my business affairs. In fact, he saved my business. A recovered Catholic priest talked to me and that helped. I finally caved in. My last day in a treatment center, I decided my days were numbered. What scared me the most was not the thought of dying, but the thought of going crazy. Fear of losing my mental capacities and functions, of losing my mind, was the big issue. I joined AA on July 4, 1975 after a disastrous drunk the day before. I got mad at my brother-in-law and got stinking drunk. I guess that showed him!

But I quit the next day and with the help of AA, I've been sober ever since. Sobriety has been good for me. My business has prospered, I've managed to find a way to help thousands of alcoholics and their families, and I've stayed sober. I am a successful businessman, but the real success of my life was my victory over alcoholism. I'm a grateful recovered alcoholic and I plan to stay that way one day at a time.

The Twelve Steps
of Alcoholics Anonymous

1. We admitted we were powerless over alcohol—that our lives had become unmanageable.
2. Came to believe that a Power greater than ourselves could restore us to sanity.
3. Made a decision to turn our will and our lives over to the care of God *as we understood Him.*
4. Made a searching and fearless moral inventory of ourselves.
5. Admitted to God, to ourselves, and to another human being the exact nature of our wrongs.
6. Were entirely ready to have God remove all these defects of character.
7. Humbly asked Him to remove our shortcomings.
8. Made a list of all persons we had harmed, and became willing to make amends to them all.
9. Made direct amends to such people wherever possible, except when to do so would injure them or others.
10. Continued to take personal inventory and when we were wrong promptly admitted it.
11. Sought through prayer and meditation to improve our conscious contact with God *as we understood Him,* praying only for knowledge of His will for us and the power to carry that out.
12. Having had a spiritual awakening as the result of these steps, we tried to carry this message to alcoholics, and to practice these principles in all our affairs.

The Twelve Traditions of Alcoholics Anonymous

1. Our common welfare should come first; personal recovery depends upon AA unity.
2. For our group purpose there is but one ultimate authority—a loving God as He may express Himself in our group conscience. Our leaders are but trusted servants; they do not govern.
3. The only requirement for AA membership is a desire to stop drinking.
4. Each group should be autonomous except in matters affecting other groups or AA as a whole.
5. Each group has but one primary purpose—to carry its message to the alcoholic who still suffers.
6. An AA group ought never endorse, finance, or lend the AA name to any related facility or outside enterprise, lest problems of money, property, and prestige divert us from our primary purpose.
7. Every AA group ought to be fully self-supporting, declining outside contributions.
8. Alcoholics Anonymous should remain forever nonprofessional, but our service centers may employ special workers.
9. AA, as such, ought never be organized; but we may create service boards or committees directly responsible to those they serve.
10. Alcoholics Anonymous has no opinion on outside issues; hence the AA name ought never be drawn into public controversy.
11. Our public relations policy is based on attraction rather than promotion; we need always maintain personal anonymity at the level of press, radio, and films.
12. Anonymity is the spiritual foundation of all our Traditions, ever reminding us to place principles before personalities.

References, Notes, and Recommended Readings

Chapter 1. The Disease is Costly

1. DeLuca, J. and Wallace, J. *The Fourth Special Report to the United States Congress on Alcohol and Health.* National Institute on Alcohol, Alcohol Abuse and Alcoholism; Alcohol, Drug Abuse and Mental Health Administration; Rockville, MD, 1981.

2. Fein, R. *Alcohol in America: The Price We Pay.* Newport Beach, CA: Care Institute, 1984.

3. Jones, K. R. and Vischi, T. R. "Impact of Alcohol, Drug Abuse and Mental Health Treatment on Medical Care Utilization: A Review of the Research Literature," *Medical Care,* 17, No. 2, Supplement (Dec. 1979).

4. Research Triangle Institute. *Economic Costs to Society of Alcohol and Drug Abuse and Mental Illness.* Available from the Division of Planning and Policy Analysis, ADAMHA, Room 13c-15, Parklawn Building, 5600 Fishers Lane, Rockville, MD 20857.

Chapter 2. Alcoholism Doesn't Make Sense

1. *Alcoholics Anonymous.* The third edition of the "Big Book" of AA. Available from Alcoholics Anonymous World Services, Inc., P. O. Box 459, Grand Central Station, New York, N.Y. 10163.

2. Johnson, V. *I'll Quit Tomorrow.* New York: Harper & Row, 1980.

3. Wallace, J. "Alcoholism from the Inside-Out: A Phenomenological Analysis," *Alcoholism: Development, Consequences, and Interventions.* ed. N. J. Estes and M. Heinemann. St. Louis: C. V. Mosby, 1981.

Chapter 3. The Illness is Fourfold

1. *Alcoholics Anonymous.* See the Foreword by Dr. William Silkworth, "The Doctor's Opinion."

2. Foreman, R. *How to Control Your Allergies.* New York: Larchmont Books, 1979.

3. Mackarness, R. *Eating Dangerously.* New York: Harcourt, Brace, Jovanovich, 1976.

4. Rinkel, H. J., Randolph, T. G., and Zeller, M. *Food Allergy.* Springfield, IL: Charles C. Thomas, 1951.

5. Randolph, T. G. *Human Ecology and Susceptibility to the Chemical Environment*. Springfield, IL: Charles C. Thomas, 1962.

6. Selye, H. *The Stress of Life*. New York: McGraw-Hill, 1956.

Chapter 4. New Light on the Disease

1. Blum, K., Hamilton, M., Hirst, M., and Wallace, J. "Putative role of isoquinoline alkaloids in alcoholism: a link to opiates," *Alcoholism: Clinical and Experimental Research*, Vol. 2 (1978), 113-120.

2. Borg, S., Kvande, H., and Rydberg, U., *et al.* "Endorphin levels in human cerebrospinal fluid during alcohol intoxication and withdrawal," *Psychopharmacology*, 78 (1982), 101-103.

3. Burov, Yu. V. *et al.* "Effect of brain enkephalin concentration in rats with different levels of alcohol motivation," *Journal of Experimental Biology and Medicine* (1983), 936-939.

4. Feldman, R. S. and Quenzer, L. F. *Fundamentals of Neuropsychopharmacology*. Sunderland, MA: Sinauer Associates, Inc., 1984. An excellent comprehensive text of recent general scientific work on neurotransmitters.

5. Genazzani, A. R. *et al.* "Central deficiency of beta-endorphin in alcohol addicts," *Journal of Clinical Endocrinology and Metabolism*, Vol. 55 (1982), 583-586.

6. Gold, M. S., Pottash, A. C., Sweeney, D. R., and Kleber, H. D. "Opiate withdrawal using Clonidine: a safe, effective, and rapid nonopiate treatment," *Journal of the American Medical Association*, Vol. 243 (1980), 343-346.

7. Goldstein, D. B. *Pharmacology of Alcohol*. New York: Oxford University Press, 1983.

8. Green, A. R. and Costain, D. W. *Pharmacology and Biochemistry of Psychiatric Disorders*. New York: John Wiley, 1981. See this book for a comprehensive discussion of neurotransmitters and mental illness, alcoholism, and drug dependence.

9. Myers, R. D. and Melchoir, C. L. "Role of serontonin in alcoholism," *Serontonin in Health and Disease*. ed. W. B. Essman. New York: Spectrum, 1977, 373-430.

10. Myers, R. D. "Tetrahydroisoquinolines in the brain: the basis of an animal model of alcoholism," *Alcoholism: Clinical and Experimental Research*, Vol. 2 (1978), 145-154.

11. Myers, R D., McCaleb, M. L., and Ruwe, W. D. "Alcohol drinking induced in the monkey by tetrahydropapaveroline (THP) infused into the cerebral ventricle," *Pharmacology, Biochemistry, and Behavior*, Vol. 16 (1982), 995-1000. Consult for new research on brain condensation products.

12. Naranjo, C. *et al.* "Zimelidine-induced variations in alcohol intake by

non-depressed heavy drinkers," *Clinical Pharmacology Therapy*, (March 1984), 374-380. See this report for a possible role of serotonin in attenuating heavy drinking.

13. Restak, R. M. *The Brain: The Lost Frontier.* New York: Warner Books, 1979. An excellent book for the general reader seeking an understanding of the brain.

14. Sweeney, D. R., Gold, M. S., Ryan, N., Pottash, A.L.C. "Opiate withdrawal and panic anxiety," *Scientific Proceedings of the 133rd Annual Meeting of the American Psychiatric Association*, 1980, 123-124 (abstract).

Chapter 5. Other Problems

1. Andreasen, N. C. *The Broken Brain: The Biological Revolution in Psychiatry.* New York: Harper & Row, 1984. See this book for an excellent general discussion of the biological bases for many psychiatric disorders.

2. Baldessarini, R. J. *Biomedical Aspects of Depression and Its Treatment.* Washington: American Psychiatric Press, 1983. See this book for a discussion of how antidepressant medications are thought to work.

3. Braestrup, C. *et al.* "Beta-carboline-3-carboxylates and benzodiazepine receptors," *GABA and Benzodiazepine Receptors.* ed. Costa, E., Dichiara, G., and Gessa, G. New York: Raven Press, 1981.

4. Davis, J. M. and Maas, J. W. *The Affective Disorders.* Washington: American Psychiatric Press, 1983.

5. Folkenberg, J. "Biochemistry of Anxiety," *ADHAMA News* (June 13, 1982).

6. Kovalesky, A. "Mitral Valve Prolapse," *Nursing 81* (April 1981), 58-61.

7. Nadi, N. S., Nurnberger, J. I., and Gershon, E. S. "Muscarinic cholinergic receptors on skin fibroblasts in familial affective disorder," *New England Journal of Medicine*, Vol. 311 (July 1984), 225-230. See this article for recent research on the genetic transmission of manic-depressive illness.

8. Redmond, D. E., and Huang, D. X. "New evidence for a locus ceruleus-norepinephrine connection with anxiety," *Life Sciences*, 25 (1979), 2149-2162.

9. Skolnick, P. and Paul, S. "New concepts in the neurobiology of anxiety," *Journal of Clinical Psychiatry*, 44 (November 1983), 12-20.

10. Sweeney, D. R., Pottash, A.L.C., Gold, M.S., and Martin D. "Panic anxiety: tricyclic antidepressant levels and clinical response," *Scientific Proceedings of the 134th Annual Meeting of the American Psychiatric Association*, 1981, 220-201 (abstract).

11. Turner, S. M. and Hersen, M. *Adult Psychopathology and Diagnosis.* New York: Wiley, 1984. An excellent general text on psychiatric problems.

Chapter 6. A Family Disease

1. *Alateen: Hope for Children of Alcoholics.* New York: Al-Anon Family Group Headquarters, 1980.

2. *Living With an Alcoholic with the Help of Al-Anon.* New York: Al-Anon Family Group Headquarters, 1980.

3. Black, C. *It Will Never Happen to Me.* Hollywood, FL: Health Communications (2119-A Hollywood Boulevard, Hollywood, FL 33020). See this book for a discussion of children of alcoholics.

4. Cloninger, C. R. "Genetic and environmental factors in the development of alcoholism," *Journal of Psychiatric Treatment and Evaluation,* Vol. 5 (1983), 487-496.

5. Cloninger, C. R., Bohman, M., and Siguardsson, S. "Inheritance of alcohol abuse: cross-fostering analysis of adopted men," *Archives of General Psychiatry,* Vol. 38 (1981), 861-969.

6. Goodwin, D. W. *et al.* "Alcohol problems in adoptees raised apart from alcoholic biological parents," *Archives of General Psychiatry,* Vol. 28 (1973), 238-243.

7. Wallace, J. "Personality Disturbances Before and After the Onset of Alcoholism," *Focus on Family,* U.S. Journal of Drug and Alcohol Dependence (2119-A Hollywood Boulevard, Hollywood, FL 33020).

8. Wegscheider, S. *Another Chance: Hope and Health for the Alcoholic Family.* Palo Alto: Science and Behavior Books, Inc., 1981.

Chapter 7. Sobriety: The Renewal of Self

1. Arky, R. A. "The effect of alcohol on carbohydrate metabolism: carbohydrate metabolism in alcoholics," *The Biology of Alcoholism,* Vol. 1. ed. B. Kissin and H. Begleiter. New York: Plenum Press, 1971.

2. Beard, J. and Knott, D. H. "The effect of alcohol on fluid and electrolyte metabolism," *The Biology of Alcoholism,* Vol. 1.

3. Butters, N. "The Wernicke-Korsakoff Syndrome," *Biomedical Processes and Consequences of Alcohol Use.* DHHS Pub. No. (ADM) 82-1191, pp. 257-287. Washington, D.C. Supt. of Docs., 1982.

4. DeLuca, J. and Wallace, J. *Fourth Special Report to the U.S. Congress on Alcohol and Health.* Washington, DC: Alcohol, Drug Abuse, and Mental Health Administration, 1981. See Chapter III for a discussion of studies showing improvement in neuropsychological functioning with sobriety.

5. Edmondson, H. A. *et al.* "Renal papillary necrosis with special reference to chronic alcoholism: a report of twenty cases," *Archives of Internal Medicine,* 118 (1966), 225-264.

6. Fuster, V. *et al.* "The natural history of idiopathic dilated cardio-

myopathy," *American Journal of Cardiology*, 47 (1981), 525-531.

7. Greenspoon, A. J., Leier, C. B., and Schaal, S. F. "Acute ethanol effects on cardiac arrhythmias and conduction in man" (abstract), *Clinical Research*, 29 (1981), 200A.

8. Leevy, C. M., Tanribilar, A. K., and Smith, F. S. "Biochemistry of gastrointestinal and liver disease in alcoholism," *The Biology of Alcoholism*, Vol. 1. ed. B. Kissin and H. Begleiter. New York: Plenum Press, 1971.

9. Leier, C. V. *et al.* "Heart block in alcoholic cardiomyopathy," *Archives of Internal Medicine*, 134 (1974), 766-768.

10. Lieber, C. S., Rubin, E., and DeCarli, L. M. "Effects of ethanol on lipid, uric acid, intermediary, and drug metabolism, including the parthogenesis of the alcoholic fatty liver," *The Biology of Alcoholism*, Vol. 1. ed. B. Kissin and H. Begleiter. New York: Plenum Press, 1971.

11. Ron, M. A. *et al.* "Computerized tomography of the brain in chronic alcoholism: a survey and follow-up study," *Brain*, 105 (1982), 497-514.

12. Van Thiel, D. H. and Lester, R. "Alcoholism: its effect on hypothalamic-pituitary-gonadal function," *Gastroenterology*, 71 (1976), 318-327.

Chapter 8. Not Only in Bottles

1. Bennett, G., Vourakis, C., and Woolf, D. S., Eds. *Substance Abuse: Pharmacologic, Developmental, and Clinical Perspectives.* New York: Wiley, 1983. Highly recommended reading for those interested in the general topic of drug dependence.

2. Cohen, S. *The Substance Abuse Problems.* New York: Haworth Press, 1981. An excellent overview of drug dependence of all types.

3. Rosenberg, J. M. *Prescriber's Guide to Drug Interactions.* Oradell, NJ: Medical Economics Co. (Book Division), 1978.

4. Smith, D. E. "Diagnostic treatment and aftercare approaches to cocaine abuse," *Journal of Substance Abuse Treatment*, Vol. 1 (1984), 5-9.

5. Sorensen, S. M. *et al.* "Persistent effects of amphetamine on cerebellar purkinje neurons following chronic administration," *Brain Research*, Vol. 247 (1982), 365-371.

Chapter 9. Alcoholism at Work

1. Califano, J. *The 1982 Report on Drug Abuse and Alcoholism.* New York: Warner Books, 1982.

2. Jones, K. R. and Vischi, T. R. "Impact of alcohol, drug abuse, and mental health treatment on medical care utilization: a review of the research literature," *Medical Care*, 17 (December 1979).

Chapter 10. What to Expect from Treatment

1. DeLuca, J. and Wallace, J. *The Fourth Special Report to the U.S. Congress on Alcohol and Health.* Rockville, MD: Alcohol, Drug Abuse, and Mental Health Administration, 1981. See Chapter VII, "Treatment and Rehabilitation," for a complete discussion of issues in alcoholism treatment.

2. Eckardt, M. *et al.* "Biochemical diagnosis of alcoholism," *Journal of the American Medical Association,* Vol. 246 (1981), 2707-2710.

3. Mandell, M. "The diagnostic value of therapeutic fasting and food ingestion tests in a controlled environment," *Journal of the International Academy of Metabology* (March 1975), 83.

4. Pendery, M., Maltzman, I., and West, L. J. "Controlled drinking by alcoholics? New findings and a reevaluation of a major affirmative study," *Science,* Vol. 217 (1982), 169-175.

5. Philpott, W. A. "The significance of selective food and chemical stressors in ecological hypoglycemia and hyperglycemia as demonstrated by induction testing techniques," *Journal of the International Academy of Metabology,* Vol. V, No. 1, p. 81.

6. Widman, F. K. *Clinical Interpretation of Laboratory Tests.* 8th edition. Philadelphia: Davis Company, 1979.

7. Zimberg, S., Wallace, J., and Blume, S. *Practical Approaches to Alcoholism Psychotherapy.* 2nd ed. New York: Plenum Press, 1985. This is a comprehensive text on all aspects of alcoholism counseling and therapy.

Chapter 11. The Reality Principle: Surrender Sets Us Free

1. *The Twelve Steps and Twelve Traditions.* Alcoholics Anonymous World Services. See especially Chapters 1, 2 and 3, which consider the first three steps to recovery through surrender.

Chapter 12. In Search of Self

1. Silverstein, L. *Consider the Alternative.* Minneapolis: Compcare Publications (2415 Annapolis Lane, Suite 140, Minneapolis, MN 55441), 1977.

Chapter 13. Alcoholics Anonymous: Myths and Realities

1. *Alcoholics Anonymous.* 3rd ed. of the AA "Big Book." Alcoholics Anonymous World Services, Inc., P. O. Box 459, Grand Central Station, New York, NY 10163.

2. Kurtz, E. "Why AA works: the intellectual significance of Alcoholics Anonymous," *Journal of Studies on Alcohol,* Vol. 43 (1982), 38-80.

3. *Twelve Steps and Twelve Traditions.* Alcoholics Anonymous World Services, at address above.

4. Wallace, J. "Ideology, belief, and behavior: Alcoholics Anonymous as a social movement," *Etiological Aspects of Alcohol and Drug Abuse.* ed. E. Gottheil et al. Springfield: Charles C. Thomas, 1983.

5. Wallace, J. "Myths and Misconceptions about Alcoholics Anonymous," *About AA* (Spring 1984). Alcoholics Anonymous World Services, at address above.

Index